MW00719000

I CAN
STAND ON
MOUNTAINS

I CAN STAND ON MOUNTAINS

A BOOK OF ENCOURAGEMENT
AND CHALLENGE

DAN MANNINGHAM

Ambassador International
GREENVILLE, SOUTH CAROLINA & BELFAST, NORTHERN IRELAND

www.ambassador-international.com

I Can Stand on Mountains

© 2016 by Dan Manningham

All rights reserved

ISBN: 978-1-62020-579-2

eISBN: 978-1-62020-654-6

All Scripture quotations, unless otherwise indicated, are taken from the Holy Bible, New International Version®. NIV® Copyright © 1973, 1978, 1984 by International Bible Society. Used by permission of Zondervan. All rights reserved.

Scripture marked ASV is taken from the Holy Bible, American Standard Version, which is in the public domain.

Scripture marked ESV is taken from the Holy Bible, English Standard Version Copyright © 2001 by **Crossway Bibles, a publishing ministry of Good News Publishers.**

Scripture marked ISV is taken from the Holy Bible, International Standard Version Copyright © 1995-2014 by **ISV Foundation**. All rights reserved internationally. Used by permission of **Davidson Press, LLC.**

Scripture marked MSG is taken from *The Message* Copyright © 1993, 1994, 1995, 1996, 2000, 2001, 2002 by **Eugene H. Peterson.**

Underlined portions of Scripture indicate emphasis added by the author.

Cover Design & Typesetting by Hannah Nichols
Ebook Conversion by Anna Riebe Raats

Ambassador International
411 University Ridge, Suite B14
Greenville, SC 29601
www.ambassador-international.com

AMBASSADOR BOOKS
The Mount
2 Woodstock Link
Belfast, BT6 8DD, Northern Ireland, UK
www.ambassadormedia.co.uk

The colophon is a trademark of Ambassador

To Fran. My navigator and my anchor, both, for 57 years.

CONTENTS

FOREWORD

Faith sees the invisible, believes the unbelievable and receives the impossible.

—Corrie ten Boom

The Sovereign Lord is my strength;

he makes my feet like the feet of a deer,

he enables me to tread on the heights.

Habakkuk 3:19

THIS BOOK IS INTENDED TO be a source of encouragement and challenge. It explores several of the specific mountains mentioned in the Bible but with the purpose always being to find in those historic peaks the unique message each of them brings. All of the important geology here is spiritual and personal because *He enables me to tread on the heights.*

The Bible is filled with symbols, and we miss much of its depth and richness without understanding those symbols. *Sheep* are frequently figures of weakness and gullibility—defenseless creatures in need of guidance, like us. The *heart* is a symbol of our innermost being: our thoughts and intents and emotions. *Light* is often a symbol of God's Word, a beacon for us to follow and an illumination of life's complexities. These are all rich symbols and each could easily be the basis of a book, but here I intend to focus on the meaning of God's mountains.

But not mountains in general. It is almost a cliché among biblical scholars (of which I am surely not one) that mountains and hills in general are a symbol of nations, earthly powers: Babylon, Assyria, Egypt, and such. This is a nice insight, but it is my intent to examine not mountains as a general symbol, but individual mountains (and hills) for their individual meaning in our Christian lives: Ararat, Moriah, Sinai, Ebal, Gilead, Carmel, Gilboa, Golgotha, Mars Hill, Gerizim, and Zion. Each one of these real and identifiable mountains has a rich story and out of that story a profound meaning for our daily lives because God has promised that He *enables me to tread on the heights.*

If that is true, what are those heights, those mountains and hills? What would it mean for me to stand on spiritual mountains? Is it just some platitude without any serious foundation? Or is there some substance to that concept?

I think there is substance and I think we can find the answers to all of those questions. We can live above the valleys of life, but equally important, we must stand on the right mountains. Many of the mountains mentioned in Scripture were powerful symbols of specific spiritual promises. There is meaning to these heights and I want to know what it is.

But some of those biblical heights were mentioned as a warning to Israel and to us. Some of the high places were places of idol worship because people have always been drawn to heights but not always to the right ones. Counterfeit heights abound: gossip, alcohol, TV, sex, criticism, drugs, excessive recreation, and the biggest of all—self.

This is nothing new. Ezekiel warned the Jews six hundred years before Christ, "When I brought them into the land I had sworn to give them and they saw any high hill or any leafy tree, there they offered their sacrifices, made offerings that provoked me to anger, presented their fragrant incense and poured out their drink offerings. Then I said to them: What is this high place you go to?" (Ezekiel 20:28-29). This is a question I need to address in relation to my favorite high hill.

God had designated the mountains and hills He wanted for the Jews to remember and on which to worship but they—like we—found other options. Mountain heights are alluring, but we want to always determine which ones God intended for our spiritual maturity.

The highlands described in this book are peaks, which stand as resolute symbols of our relationship with God and God's law. Some are symbols of His mercy and goodness, of personal victory, sacrifice, and courage; and some are symbols of warning and danger.

You can stand on the right mountains. You don't have to live in the valleys. You don't have to continue worshiping tawdry personal idols on puny little hills. And you don't have to waste your time climbing dangerous and destructive mountains. With God's help you can stand on His mountains. He said so.

> *"Come, let us go up to the mountain of the Lord,*
>
> *to the house of the God of Jacob.*
>
> *He will teach us his ways,*
>
> *so that we may walk in his paths."*

Micah 4:2b

INTRODUCTION

You raise me up so I can stand on mountains.

—Brendan Graham

I lift up my eyes to the hills—
where does my help come from?
My help comes from the Lord,
the Maker of heaven and earth.

Psalm 121:1–2

WHEN I WAS FOUR YEARS old, in the summer of 1941, I climbed Welch Mountain in the Waterville Valley of New Hampshire with my family. Welch Mountain is not big as mountains go, a mere 2,605 feet above sea level, about the size of the Mount of Olives near Jerusalem, but it is a lovely place for a day hike and the summit is a bare rock, which offers wonderful views of the deep valley below and the Mad River that defines that valley. It is also a great place to pick wild blueberries in season if the black bears and birds don't find them first. But the greatest joy is sitting on the crown of Welch in summer sunshine and savoring the vistas of the Sandwich Range and the Waterville Valley. It is a fine place to gain perspective on heights and depths, mountains and valleys, hopes and fears.

On the seventy-fifth anniversary of that excursion in 2016, I climbed Welch again as a personal mission of delight to celebrate the many years I have enjoyed visits to that part of New England and the vague but real memory of that first ascent as a young boy. That anniversary climb proved to be as enjoyable and meaningful as the first.

Mountains are magnificent creations of an ingenious and artistic God. They are glorious sculptures of rock and soil, trees and flowers, moss and lichen that decorate the surface of the earth with splendid texture. In forty-five years of flying over five continents, I have seen nothing to compare with the mountains of Greenland, the Rockies of North America, the European Alps, the Wamena Range of central Papua, the Alaska Range, the Hindu Cush of central Asia, as well as the more gentle and green slopes of Scotland's Highlands and the American Appalachians.

But mountains also have great practical value. Mountains form about one fourth of the earth's landmass and directly impact the lives of much of the earth's population. Mountains significantly affect weather by squeezing water from the atmosphere on the windward side and sheltering the leeward side from wet weather. This action produces a great proportion of the world's available fresh water, which drains down the windward sides of mountain ranges into magnificent rivers which then go on to irrigate much of the world's food supply while also providing much-needed water for human consumption and hygiene. And the leeward side of those ranges produces fertile grasslands that are excellent for grain crops and livestock.

Some of those mountains produce vast atmospheric waves ("mountain waves") that reach upward as much as fifteen miles, stirring the air and distributing its thermal components upward to great heights, thus creating atmospheric stability that can prevent even greater storms than what we already experience.

Mountains are conduits to population movement and protection from enemies. They control the flow of animal migration and provide shelter and refuge for many species. Geologically speaking, they are significant because they document the natural history of the region by exposing multiple layers of uplifted material.

And in a similar way, God's chosen mountains, the ones we read about in Scripture, have practical messages and valuable meaning for those who have determined to live a life pleasing to God.

The mountains are God's thoughts piled up.

—Sam Jones

He who forms the mountains . . .

and treads the high places of the earth—

the Lord God Almighty is his name.

Amos 4:13

Truly, God has "piled up" an anthology of priceless thoughts in His descriptions and His purposes for mountains in the Bible. They are more than big hills with names. Mountains are mentioned more than five hundred times in the Bible. Often they represent places where select individuals can be closer to God: Abraham on Moriah; Moses on Sinai; Elijah on Carmel; Jesus on the Mount of Transfiguration. In many cases, they are symbols of His desires and precepts and hopes for His people.

Noah and his family of eight came to rest on Mount Ararat, a symbol of God's deliberate choice to save one family of believers from His wrath.

Mount Moriah was the place where Abraham was tested by God by being commanded to sacrifice his son Isaac; and it is the place where Abraham set an example of faith for all succeeding generations and where God displayed His great love of obedience.

Mount Sinai was the location chosen by God to hand down His ten great decrees for living that are known as the Ten Commandments and remain, today, the foundation of all civilized law.

In the New Testament, Jesus was tempted on a mountain, He delivered His most significant sermon "on the Mount," He gave His parting message to the church on the Mount of Olives and He commissioned His apostles on a mountain.

And then there is Golgotha, that insignificant hill outside of Jerusalem on which the very Son of God, the perfect Lamb, died for my sins, and yours.

He who formed the mountains is mighty indeed. And His mountains are majestic symbols of His character and nature. For that reason, it is a grand adventure to explore God's mountains in Scripture and find in them the messages they contain.

Climb the mountains
and get their good tidings.

—John Muir

The Lord, the Lord Almighty, has a day
of tumult and trampling and terror
in the Valley of Vision,
a day of battering down walls
and of crying out to the mountains.

Isaiah 22:5

It is the nature of men and women to live in the valleys. Isaiah knew that when he coined the term *Valley of Vision.* We are a race given to petty issues, personal desires, and fear and worry and anxiety. Without some conscious effort, we just live in the valleys. It is easy because gravity works, even spiritual and emotional gravity.

Still, those who see Christ as Lord and Savior are more precious to the heart of God—each one of us—than entire galaxies of suns and moons and planets. For this very reason, we ought to strive for a view from the top, a view from the mountains, a view above this Valley of Vision. When we stand high, we can see far.

When the apostle John was an old man, he was exiled to the remote island of Patmos in the Aegean Sea. There he was given a vision of things that would happen at the end of time, a vision that we read in the book of Revelation. In chapter 21 of that book, when God reveals the wonder and majesty of His eternal kingdom, He *carried [John] away to a mountain great and high* (v. 10) for the viewing of those holy and eternal things. It was from that mountaintop that John could see the vista of God's plan for eternity. And it is from other mountains that we gain a right perspective of our holy calling. God's mountains have wonderful significance and meaning. They are there for all who will climb.

> Today is your day!
> Your mountain is waiting.
> So . . . get on your way.
>
> —Dr. Seuss

> *As the mountains surround Jerusalem, so the Lord surrounds his people both now and forevermore.*
>
> Psalm 125:2

Finally, there seems to be importance to the sequence—the order—of God's mountain revelations. There is the clear *choice* by God to save Noah and his family from *wrath* (Ararat), the introduction of *obedience by faith* (Moriah) as the one thing above all others that pleases Him, the giving of the Ten Commandments as His *covenant of holy living* (Sinai), the reminder of God's *power for victory* (Carmel), the great demonstration of His *grace and our redemption* (Golgotha), and the command to *evangelize* a world that is spiritually lost and dying amid intellectual chaos (Mars Hill).

In the end, it is obvious that God loves mountains and that He uses them as teaching points in His great plan for humanity.

We can stand on mountains. He said so in Psalm 18:33 and elsewhere. And it is helpful to understand those peaks and how they represent critical aspects of our spiritual life in Christ.

Let's climb.

> The Beauty of the Mountain is hidden for all those who try to discover it from the top, supposing that, one way or another, one can reach this place directly. The Beauty of the Mountain is revealed only to those who have climbed it.
>
> —Antoine de Saint-Exupéry

> *Who may ascend the hill of the Lord?*
> *Who may stand in his holy place?*
> *He who has clean hands and a pure heart.*
>
> Psalm 24:3–4a

CHAPTER ONE

THE JOYS OF CLIMBING

Why should we live halfway up the hill and swathed in mists, when we might have an unclouded sky and a radiant sun over our heads if we would climb higher and walk in the light of His face?

—Alexander Maclaren

The path of life leads upward for the wise.

Proverbs 15:24a

GRAVITY IS A POWERFUL FORCE. It draws things down to the lowest possible level, and spiritual gravity does the same thing in the spiritual realm. Everything struggles with gravity; that is the very reason that climbing mountains is challenging.

And yet there are some things that persist and overcome that pull of gravity. I have a lovely plant in my front yard, a *Mandevilla* plant that begins each summer at a height of about twelve inches because I cut it back every fall and store it for the winter. During the early summer, this plant grows and attaches itself to a trellis and quickly overcomes gravity to reach eight feet in height and it would grow much higher if I let it. Along the way, this lovely *Mandevilla* generates multiple blossoms that celebrate its long climb with brilliant white punctuations. The whole thing is a triumph over gravity and a testimony to beauty in the midst of struggle. Some things heroically resist the difficult burden of gravity.

I have watched my grandchildren toddle over to their dad and struggle to climb onto his knee and then scramble again to climb to his face because gravity is no match for a child's love of his father. Some things resist the pull of gravity.

And, I have watched marriages and lives weighed down by anger and unforgiveness and selfishness climb that Jacob's ladder of prayer and forgiveness and gritty spiritual work to new heights of healing. Some things and some people repel the pull of gravity and when they employ the power of God in the process, they are assured of a good result.

> You say, "I am afraid I cannot hold out."
> Well, Christ will hold out for you. There is no mountain that He will not climb with you if you will; He will deliver you from your besetting sin.
>
> —D. L. Moody

> *He makes my feet like the feet of a deer;*
> *He enables me to stand on the heights.*
>
> Psalm 18:33

The highest mountain in the northeast US is Mount Washington in the state of New Hampshire. It is not great as world mountains go, but at 6,288 feet it dominates the local topography and is large enough that very early explorers could see the mountain from the Atlantic Ocean over a hundred miles away when the weather was clear.

Mount Washington does have another distinction. It is host to some of the most erratic and severe weather on earth. For seventy-six years, until 2010, the weather observatory on the summit held the record for the highest wind gust directly recorded on the earth's surface, 231 mph on April 12, 1934. Even in mid-summer, the weather on Washington can be treacherous and temperature drops of forty degrees and more have been recorded between the base and the summit. In October 2008, *Backpacker Magazine* listed Mount Washington as one of America's ten most dangerous hikes.

But there are several ways to reach the summit of this majestic mountain. There are at least six well-developed and well-marked hiking trails, each requiring a solid one-day hike to get to the summit and back. Start early because it will take longer than you think unless you are an experienced New England hiker.

There is a 7.6-mile toll road that is navigable by almost any car in reasonable condition.

And there is a cog railway that travels up a three-mile line that is the steepest railway in the United States. It is so steep that the old steam engine passes over cogs that are like one long ratchet designed to hold the train in place in the event of engine or brake failure. It is a great ride especially on a clear day—scenic, historic, and pleasant.

So, if you want to experience the wonder of standing at the summit of Mount Washington, you have three options: two that require little or no effort and one that requires determination, perseverance, and careful preparation. The hike is tiring, but it is exhilarating and greatly satisfying, as are most mountain hikes.

I am sure that God made no mistake when He commanded Moses to climb Mount Sinai to receive the Ten Commandments instead of miraculously transporting him to the summit. The long climb up that steep mountain surely was a metaphor of the moral and spiritual climb God desires for all of us. It is not an allegory of working out our salvation, since salvation is available only as a free gift by an exercise of faith. But it does appear to be an expression of God's desire that we be willing to climb higher in an effort to draw closer to Him, as in, *"If you love me, you will obey what I command"* (John 14:15) and, *Do not merely listen to the word, and so deceive yourselves. Do what it says* (James 1:22).

And so, Moses climbed. And Moses, who was already a chosen and beloved child of God, persisted in that long, tiring physical climb because God had called him. Yes, there was a mountain to climb, but there was joy in the obedience of climbing, even if the effort was difficult.

The closer you live to God,

the smaller everything else appears.

—Rick Warren

I confess my iniquity; I am troubled by my sin.

Psalm 38:18

Mountain climbing is often hazardous. Smaller mountains like those in New England are normally pleasant and enjoyable, even for children when accompanied by adults and with simple preparations. I have seen parents backpacking with infants and children as young as three enjoying a day hike on smaller mountains. But there are hazards. Hikers occasionally fail to dress appropriately, start too late in the day, or stumble on the uneven terrain and injure themselves. Several times a year the 911 centers receive calls from hikers who are lost or stranded, even on relatively benign trails. Some of those find themselves in trouble due to their own foolishness. They will be rescued, but they are likely to receive a bill for hundreds or thousands of dollars from the state of New Hampshire if they have been seriously irresponsible.

Mount Everest is at the other end of the scale in terms of difficulty and danger. This highest mountain on the planet has seen over two hundred deaths, about 4 percent of all those who have climbed to the peak. Everest is for serious risk takers, but it seems to be irresistible for those who find themselves with a hunger for true excitement and challenge—and that is true to varying degrees with all mountains. They all provide some level of challenge and excitement.

But the challenge begins when we realize that our natural habitat is in the lowlands. The excitement of climbing is the result of seeing the difference between where we are and where we could be. As J. C. Ryle said, *"The first step toward attaining a higher standard of holiness is to realize more fully the amazing sinfulness of sin."*

That recognition of our sinfulness is the great motivation to begin a spiritual climb, just as living in the valleys is motivation to see the world from a higher vantage and to see just how small everything else is. There is great joy in climbing. Great effort and great joy.

If we will, there is also companionship, instruction, assistance, and guidance. The mountains beckon, those that are physical and those that are spiritual.

> Satan tempts us to live a low life,
> but God tempts us to come up higher.
>
> —Joyce Meyer

> *Who may ascend the hill of the Lord?*
> *Who may stand in his holy place?*
> *He who has clean hands and a pure heart.*
>
> Psalm 24:3-4a

CHAPTER TWO

ARARAT: MOUNTAIN OF WRATH AND MERCY

I like being near the top of a mountain.
One can't get lost here.

—Wislawa Szymborska

On the seventeenth day of the seventh month the ark came to rest on the mountains of Ararat.

Genesis 8:4

MOUNT ARARAT IS ACTUALLY A range of mountains in what is today known as the Eastern Anatolian region of Turkey, close to the Iranian border. Present-day Ararat is a snow-capped, dormant volcano, which includes two peaks: Greater Ararat, 16,854 feet high, and Lesser Ararat, 12,782 feet high. Scholars may disagree about the exact geographic location where Noah's ark rests, but those academic disputes really have no relevance for the topic of this chapter.

We know from the biblical account that God destroyed the earth with a great flood and out of that He preserved eight people who survived on a great boat and ultimately landed on Ararat as the waters receded. It is reasonably certain that the Ararat of Genesis and the Ararat of modern geography are the same.

Incidentally, this story of a global flood is not unique to Judaism and Christianity. Cultures in Babylon, Persia, Greece, Africa, North and South America, Australia, and many other locales all have some version of the flood story with very similar details.

These flood tales—over five hundred worldwide—are frequently linked by common elements that parallel the biblical account, including the warning of a coming flood, the construction of a boat in advance, the rescue of animals, the inclusion of a family, and the release of birds to determine if the water level had subsided. The overwhelming consistency among flood legends found in distant parts of the globe suggests they were derived from a common origin, although oral transmission has changed some of the details through time.

It is not only a story that Christians believe by faith, but a story that has significant cultural and geological evidence to support it. In fact, even the purpose for the great flood is similar in all those varied cultures; the flood is described as God's response to pervasive immorality and violence. All of the flood legends include the same initiating cause: humankind's pervasive evil.

The biblical account says that in the days of Noah the world population was consumed with idolatry, immorality, and violence. People had drifted into utter depravity. In fact, they were so completely corrupt that God decided to end it all with an unimaginable flood that destroyed the entire human race and all they had accomplished to that time. *Now the earth was corrupt in God's sight and was full of violence. God saw how corrupt the earth had become, for all the people on earth had corrupted their ways* (Genesis 6:11–12).

The meaning of Ararat is grounded in those wicked events that led up to the flood and those events culminate in God's wrath as a righteous response to humankind's evil. The story begins with God's wrath and ends with His sovereign mercy.

Sin is not a popular topic in the twenty-first century. We have become far too comfortable with a diminished god of compassion and love and forgiveness, but absent is the holiness, majesty, and righteousness of our biblical God. It is true, of course, that God is wise and good and compassionate, but that very same God is also fundamentally holy, just, and pure. There is no stain of evil in Him and His very nature prevents Him from condoning or associating with evil. He is also a just God and therefore cannot overlook evil anymore than modern criminal justice can simply overlook rape or murder.

Ararat would never have been mentioned in the epic of human history if God were merely kind, compassionate, and forgiving. Ararat is a towering symbol of His just and righteous wrath as well as His deliverance and protection. It is both. It is a truly unique mountain.

> One of the most striking things about the Bible is the vigor with which both Testaments emphasize the reality and terror of God's wrath.
>
> —J. I. Packer

*The Lord saw how great man's wickedness on the earth had become . . .
So the Lord said, "I will wipe mankind, whom I have created, from the
face of the earth . . . for I am grieved that I have made them.*

Genesis 6:5–7

God's wrath is unlike its human counterpart. Human wrath is wayward, spontaneous, selfish, and harmful. Human wrath is the outpouring of invective, intending personal injury toward someone or something that at the moment is personally bothersome. Human wrath is seldom productive or helpful; it is more commonly injurious and nasty. Human wrath is most often an ugly and repulsive thing.

God's wrath, on the other hand, is entirely different, despite the use of that same word. It is a shame that there is not some more distinguishing term to differentiate between human and divine wrath, but in the English language we are stuck with that simple word *wrath*.

God's wrath is not some spontaneous expression of anger; it is His permanent attitude when confronted by sin and evil. It is one of His personal qualities, without which God would cease to be fully righteous and would be simply insipid and weak. God's wrath is as permanent a fixture of His character and being as His love. In Scripture you can see unambiguous examples of His wrath in the destruction of Korah's family (Numbers 16), the ten plagues on the Egyptians (Exodus 7–12), the demolition of Sodom and Gomorrah (Genesis 19), and the utter elimination of the Amalekites (1 Samuel 15). These were not spontaneous fits of anger; they were all expressions of His holy and righteous animus in response to repulsive and defiant human behavior. It is who God is. It is what God does, precisely because He is holy and just.

Mark this carefully. God's wrath is not a simple response to personal offense that we humans are so familiar with. Rather, God's wrath is a deeply rooted personal quality, a permanent and consistent part of His intrinsic nature. God's wrath is that part of His eternal and unchangeable nature that exercises judgment in the face of defiant and unrepentant evil. It is that part of His fundamental character that abhors sin and exercises justice. Finally, it is an essential part of His holiness, just as punishment in a criminal court is an essential part of justice.

Neither is God's wrath restricted to the Old Testament as some have claimed. There are not two Gods or two godly natures: cruel and punishing in the Old Testament and kind and compassionate in the New. There is one God with one nature, and that nature includes righteous wrath as an essential component of His holiness. It is a frequent theme in the New Testament even along with the incredible promises of grace, mercy, compassion, and love.

"Whoever believes in the Son has eternal life, but whoever rejects the Son will not see life, for God's wrath remains on him." *(John 3:36)*

The wrath of God is being revealed from heaven against all the godlessness and wickedness of men who suppress the truth by their wickedness. (Romans 1:18)

Let no one deceive you with empty words, for because of such things God's wrath comes on those who are disobedient. (Ephesians 5:6)

Then I heard a loud voice from the temple saying to the seven angels, "Go, pour out the seven bowls of God's wrath on the earth."
(Revelation 16:1)

And, of course, the New Testament centers on that most dramatic and cruel example of God's wrath: the crucifixion of His only begotten Son, Jesus Christ. God's wrath was exhausted on the body and spirit of the God-man Jesus in the full, excruciating pain and humiliation of Roman execution as well as the grosser pain and disgrace of separation from His Father by the filth, depravity, and corruption of the sin of all humanity.

God's wrath is an integral element of His being and nature. It is always the end result of holiness, righteousness, wisdom, and judgment. His wrath is an inevitable result of rebellion against a perfect and holy God. It is evidenced in His rejection of Lucifer, His plagues on the nation of Israel, and His devastation of Assyria, Babylon, Egypt, and countless other nations and groups that simply rejected His authority. It is, indeed, *a dreadful thing to fall into the hands of the living God* (Hebrews 10:31).

But, there is another dimension of God, which is evident in this story; it is the fact of His choosing people and nations for His reasons and for His purposes. He doesn't need to explain Himself. He is sovereign, supreme, and autonomous. He makes choices, and His purposes in those choices are not always apparent, although they are always good.

God chose Job, a thoroughly righteous man, to suffer terribly to make that very point. God is sovereign. We are not. His purposes are His alone but always for ultimate good, even if we never understand.

He chose Mary to be Jesus' mother. He chose Paul, a nasty and aggressive persecutor of Christians, to be His great messenger of grace. He chose pagan Abram to become the father of the Jewish nation. He chose Moses to be spared from infanticide and eventually be appointed leader of the entire nation despite his criminal background. He chose Assyria to punish Judah and then chose to destroy Assyria. He chooses. He does so from His infinite wisdom, goodness, justice, and sovereignty. But, in the end, He chooses and not always according to a decision process that we would recognize or approve.

In this story of the great flood, there is God's choice of Noah and his family as the survivors and progenitors of the human race. Eight people were saved out of that pandemic flood. Eight. All the rest were destroyed, and God's plan for the entire world was invested in those eight chosen people.

God chose those people in the same way He chose all believers. Theologians have debated the meaning and implication of this attribute of God since the beginning of the church, but it appears that we will never know His reasons or His methods in this life. In the end, we can only know that He makes clear and specific choices and that He makes them according to His perfect sovereignty over all matters.

God is sovereign. He is supreme. His choices are according to His purposes. I think that God would agree with Forrest Gump when he concludes his explanations with the statement, "That's all I have to say about that."

Life is God's novel. Let him write it.

—Isaac Bashevis Singer

"I am God, and there is no other;

I am God, and there is none like me.

I make known the end from the beginning, . . .

I say: My purpose will stand,

and I will do all that I please."

Isaiah 46:9b–10

HISTORY

Mount Ararat is forever etched in the lexicon of biblical stories as that place where Noah's great ark came to rest after a global, cataclysmic flood. It is the stuff of magical children's stories and even secular legend, but that mountain is one that we want to walk on because it represents deliverance from God's wrath. It is the very first mountain in God's revelation to humankind, and it is a mountain of strong meaning and significance.

Ararat reminds us that God's wrath is an integral part of His being. God's wrath is not a spontaneous and reactive work of retribution but an inherent aspect of His perfectly virtuous nature. His wrath is an essential dimension of His holy righteousness, and the expression of His wrath is always deliberate, measured, and appropriate. He cannot tolerate evil and rebellion, and His wrath is reserved for those transgressions as our criminal law incorporates punishment as an essential component of justice.

Further, there is no escape from God's wrath, except for those who are in the ark. And the ark of our age is the person of Jesus Christ. To be "in Him" is to be in the one and only ark of safety so as to be preserved from the wrath to come. *God made him who had no sin to be sin for us, so that in him we might become the righteousness of God* (2 Corinthians 5:21).

The ark—Noah's or ours—offers a place of rest, even when there seems to be no rest; even when the waters are deep; even when no relief is in sight. Under it all, there is an Ararat, where those who trust in the sovereign God will finally rest from the inevitability of His wrath in response to sin.

The ark—both Noah's and ours—is also a place identified with God's sovereign choices. Noah could never promote himself as some paragon of virtuous behavior, as his later life showed, and neither can we. Why am I sheltered in God's ark? Why was Noah? By His grace and mercy and sovereign choice. It leaves me nothing about which to boast. I am a product of His infinite mercy and grace applied by His choice.

Don't try to understand it. Just flee to the ark.

And remember the rainbow.

> The death of the Son of God and the damnation of unrepentant human beings are the loudest shouts under heaven that God is infinitely holy, and sin is infinitely offensive, and wrath is infinitely just and grace is infinitely precious.
>
> —John Piper

Whenever the rainbow appears in the clouds, I will see it and remember the everlasting covenant between God and all living creatures of every kind on the earth.

Genesis 9:16

CHAPTER THREE

MORIAH: MOUNTAIN OF FAITH AND OBEDIENCE

Faith is taking the first step
even when you don't see the whole staircase.

—Martin Luther King Jr.

Then God said, "Take your son, your only son Isaac, whom you love, and go to the region of Moriah. Sacrifice him there as a burnt offering on one of the mountains I will tell you about."

Genesis 22:2

MOUNT MORIAH IS THE NAME given to the north-south ridge of elevation lying between the Kidron Valley and Hagai Valley, between Mount Zion to the west and the Mount of Olives to the east. It ranges in elevation from about 2,000 to 2,500 feet above sea level. It is not very significant as a geological feature, but its spiritual significance and history are huge. On the peak, there is a so-called "Foundation Stone" with a small hole that enters a cavern, causing this spot to be dubbed the "Navel of the World" as if this were the place marking the birth of our planet.

Moriah has a rich history and generates some controversy. But without doubt, it stands as one of the most significant locations in biblical history and carries considerable spiritual meaning.

Some Bible scholars associate Moriah with that enigmatic priest Melchizedek, the king of Salem, who brought bread and wine to Abraham after a successful battle and to whom Abraham gave a tithe of the spoils (see Genesis 14).

Others think of Moriah as the place where Jacob slept with his head on a stone dreaming of a stairway to heaven with angels going up and down (Genesis 28).

But, the best-known and most significant event associated with Mount Moriah is the story of Abraham and Isaac, in which God commands the patriarch to sacrifice his only son by his wife Sarah. It is a story of great faith and great obedience. And that is the significance of Moriah: faith and obedience.

> Every day I put faith on the line. I have never seen God. In a world where nearly everything can be weighed, explained, quantified, subjected to psychological analysis and scientific control I persist in making the center of my life a God whom no eye has seen, nor ear heard, whose will no one can probe.
>
> —Eugene Peterson

> *And without faith it is impossible to please God, because anyone who comes to him must believe that he exists and that he rewards those who earnestly seek him.*
>
> Hebrews 11:6

John Polkinghorne is both a man of great doubts and a man of great faith. He would be more likely to tell you what he doesn't know than what he does. He is widely regarded as one of the leading thinkers of the relationship between science and faith. He received a PhD in physics from Cambridge University, is a member of the Royal Society, was president of Queens' College, won the Templeton Prize "for outstanding contributions in affirming life's spiritual dimension, whether through insight, discovery, or practical works," and he mathematically explained the existence of quarks and gluons, those mysterious, invisible, and elusive particles that science currently regards as the building blocks of matter. Oh, and he was knighted by the queen for his work in developing ethical research standards for England's scientists.

But John Polkinghorne is also a man of faith. When he was at the top of his scientific career, he left the laboratory to attend seminary because he was already believing in one unseen thing (quarks and gluons and other subatomic particles that cannot be seen but for which there is convincing mathematical evidence) in order to explore that other great unseen thing for which there is compelling evidence, namely God. The argument for quarks and gluons and God all present compelling evidence but not comprehensive proof. And in that John Polkinghorne saw something similar: a parallel between the physical and the spiritual.

In the end he became an ordained minister who believes that God exists because of the abundant evidence, in the same way that he believes that quarks exist—because of the evidence. They are both grounded in faith. They are both supported by plentiful data, and ample evidence, but they cannot be seen and in the end must be accepted by faith.

Dr. Polkinghorne, a clearly brilliant man of science and more, simply recognized what many are unwilling to admit. That we all live by faith in something: faith in God, faith in our staggering brilliance, faith in our net worth, faith in our government, faith in medicine, faith in the accumulated body of science and technology, or faith in the supposed goodness of humanity.

Exercising one's faith is part of human nature. Blaise Pascal famously said, "There is a God-shaped vacuum in the heart of every man." Pascal, who was himself a prodigious mathematician and physicist and inventor, went on to formulate what would become known as "Pascal's wager" (*Pensées,* section 233), which says that—and I paraphrase—since the existence of God cannot be proved or disproved through reason, and there is much to be gained from wagering that God exists and little to be gained from wagering that God doesn't exist, a rational person should simply wager that God exists and live accordingly. We all live by faith, so the pertinent question is not whether we have faith but just what is the object of that faith?

Such faith is the bedrock of Christianity. We believe by faith, based on solid evidence but without sufficient evidence to provide proof. (Otherwise, there would be no room for faith.) We believe in God, the atoning work of Jesus Christ, and the validity of written and canonized Scripture. And we strive to live lives of obedience that are consistent with that faith. It is all by faith, supported by an abundance of evidence.

Abraham also lived by faith and did so with such distinction that he is considered a model for all those who would do the same. Abraham knew nothing of particle physics or Pascal's wager, but he knew enough about a sovereign God to walk by faith in Him in a way that continues to resound four thousand years later. Abraham was a great man of faith because his faith was rightly anchored. But even then, Abraham's faith in the sovereign God was sorely tried when he was called to obedience on the basis of that faith on a mountain named Moriah, the mountain of faith and obedience.

> Faith and obedience are bound up in the same bundle. He that obeys God trusts God; and he that trusts God obeys God. He that is without faith is without works; and he that is without works is without faith.
>
> —Charles Spurgeon

[Jesus said,] "What do you think? There was a man who had two sons. He went to the first and said, 'Son, go and work today in the vineyard.'

"'I will not,' he answered, but later he changed his mind and went.

"Then the father went to the other son and said the same thing. He answered, 'I will, sir,' but did he did not go.

"Which of the two did what his father wanted?"

"The first," they answered.

Matthew 21:28–31a

The story of Abraham is worth reviewing because it is a story of both faith and obedience. It starts with a man named Abraham who was living in Mesopotamia in what is present-day Iraq. His precise location at that time was probably near the mouth of the Euphrates River on the Persian Gulf in a place then known as Ur.

Abraham was a pagan, possibly worshiping the moon god Nanna. He knew nothing of the one sovereign God of the Bible because there was no Bible and no oral history of the God of what later became the Bible. Nor was there any tradition or culture of monotheism. The idea of one, single God was believed to be simply preposterous.

But that very God appeared to Abraham and told him to move with all of his family to a place he did not know in order to embrace a future he could not imagine, including a family that would grow into an entire nation. This event is an established piece of biblical history but also a metaphor of what God asks of every person: "Leave your comfort zone and move into a life in which all things are new. And do that by faith."

For Abraham that meant uprooting his family and his possessions and his flocks and herds and walking a very long distance to an unfamiliar and unknown land. For us in the twenty-first century, it means an utter departure from the priorities of our secular lives and moving to an entirely new spiritual place where our priorities are reduced to loving God and loving others. We are not called to leave our jobs and communities and live in a cave, but we *are* called to a lifestyle and a worldview that are radically different from what our human, secular nature assumes. We continue to go to work, mow the lawn, coach little league, and enjoy our friends, but we do so with the faith that there is a God, that He is actively interested in our lives, and that He has a distinctive plan of action and behavior in mind for us.

We, and Abraham, share that command to walk in faith, but Abraham was a particularly good example and for that reason alone his story is valuable. It is a story that can be analyzed and dissected by scholars but also one that can be readily understood by children.

So Abraham moved with his wife and nephew and their household help to a new place called Canaan, and they settled there. There are other interludes to the story, but that is the basic event. Once settled in Canaan, Abraham and Sarah, his wife, waited for those promised children, but they didn't come until another twenty-five years passed and Abraham was a hundred years old. During those trying years, they were a man and woman of faith, waiting for God to fulfill His promise. And quite naturally, that belated son, Isaac, was the dearest thing in both of their lives. They had longed for a child and especially that child promised by God Himself, and suddenly Isaac was there. Abraham's faith had been rewarded, but it would soon be tested to the limits.

When Isaac was a boy, God spoke these words to Abraham: *"Take your son, your only son, Isaac, whom you love, and go to the region of Moriah. Sacrifice him there as a burnt offering"* (Genesis 22:2).

It is an inconceivable command to Abraham. Take your beloved son who is coincidentally the first person of a planned nation and sacrifice him as a burnt offering; sacrifice the dearest person in your life and by doing that bring the whole nation thing to an abrupt end.

But Abraham is a person of faith—and obedience. Actually, that should not be surprising because faith leads to obedience and obedience reinforces faith; they are interactive. And because Abraham is a man of both, he takes his son up the slopes of Mount Moriah, builds an altar, ties up his son, lays him on the stones, and raises his knife to make the sacrifice. At that culminating moment of faith and obedience, God intervened to spare Isaac's life and Abraham's heartache and Sarah's grief. And ever since then, Abraham has been rightly revered as a man of faith and a man of obedience.

But there can be a problem. We revere Abraham for his faith and we should. But as we do that, it is typical for us to bring Abraham down from the mountain so that his faith matches our puny faith. We think that what he did was forever beyond the faith we could demonstrate, but in truth, we should be climbing Moriah to duplicate Abraham's faith rather than bringing Abraham down to match ours. It is the very meaning of Moriah: faith and obedience.

> A string of opinions no more constitutes faith than a string of beads constitutes holiness.
>
> —John Wesley

> *Now faith is being sure of what we hope for and certain of what we do not see.*
>
> Hebrews 11:1

John Bunyan lived and wrote in the 1600s in England. He spent considerable time in jail for his straightforward, biblical teaching, and he wrote the classic *Pilgrim's Progress* while a prisoner. The book is so creative and so readable that it is still taught in English literature classes in major universities that would not otherwise include Christian classics in their curriculum. It is a wonderful read, and the various child-friendly versions and videos are great teaching aids for parents who are so inclined. Be sure to find a modern-language version.

Pilgrim's Progress is a parable of a man named Christian, who finds a book that tells him of the impending destruction of his city. The "book," of course, is the Bible and the prophesied devastation is the destruction of the world found in the book of Revelation.

So, Christian leaves his doomed City of Destruction and begins his journey, his pilgrimage, to the Celestial City, Bunyan's metaphor for heaven. Along the way, he has many adventures and difficulties—as do all who commit their lives to an obedient life of faith—but in time he reaches a river that is both wide and deep and must be crossed in order to reach the Celestial City. The river is a metaphor of death, which we all must experience and which men and women of faith must approach with faith—faith that God exists; that He has sent His Son to pay the price for their sins; that there is a Celestial City waiting for us on the other side. The river of death that all men encounter is the last, great test of faith. Even for the Christ follower, the river is a test of faith because, in spite all of the copious evidence, there is no proof and so this final experience must be approached with one final act of committed faith.

Christian is a man of great faith. Throughout the story, he has endured countless trials and seen God's hand in all of those experiences, and yet his faith wavers at the very thought of crossing the river. He nearly drowns, nearly loses his faith, but in the end he crosses that river of death with his faith intact and walks into the Celestial City. Bunyan writes, "Then they both took courage, and after that the enemy was as silent as stone, until they had crossed over. Presently Christian found ground to stand upon, and then the rest of the river was shallow. Thus they crossed over." Christian's faith was always well placed, and in the end it served him well.

At the same time, a man whose faith was in himself, a man named Ignorance, approaches the same river and crosses effortlessly in a boat piloted by another man named Vain Hope, only to fall into the entrance to hell on the other side. Both Christian and Ignorance had faith, but Ignorance's faith was in himself. And only faith in the one true God and His redeemer Son, Jesus, is effectual.

Abraham had that faith. Abraham was like Christian in leaving his personal City of Destruction and undertaking the faith journey to the city God had determined. Abraham and Christian were both men of faith and men of obedience. One was real and one was fictional, but they each teach us that important lesson for which Mount Moriah will always be known: faith demands obedience and obedience demands faith.

> "I seek an inheritance that can never perish, spoil or fade, and it is kept in heaven, to be bestowed, at the time appointed, on those who diligently seek it. Read about it in my book."
>
> —Christian, from *Pilgrim's Progress*

By faith Abraham, when called to go to a place he would later receive as his inheritance, obeyed and went, even though he did not know where he was going. By faith he made his home in the promised land like a stranger in a foreign country; . . . for he was looking forward to the city with foundations, whose architect and builder is God.

Hebrews 11:8–10

CHAPTER FOUR

SINAI: MOUNTAIN OF INSTRUCTION AND LAW

The Ten Commandments are like an 'Operator's Manual'
from the factory. The instructions are fundamental to
operation and maintenance.

—Richard Halverson

*You came down on Mount Sinai; you spoke to them from heaven. You
gave them regulations and laws that are just and right, and decrees
and commands that are good.*

Nehemiah 9:13

THE LOCATION OF MOUNT SINAI has been disputed for centuries.
Despite millennia of investigation and study, no one is really certain
of its location other than it is somewhere in Arabia. Still, if we simply
follow the biblical account of the exodus from Egypt, and the travels
of Israel, it is logical—if not provable—that Mount Sinai is in the Sinai
Peninsula, and most likely in the southern portion of that landmass. If
that is true, the mountain is about 7,500 feet in height. But regardless
of its location or size, the vital story of this mountain, God's mountain
of instruction and law, remains.

Actually, Sinai is prominent in the Old Testament story on three
very different occasions, each of those occasions being a time of godly

instruction. The first incident occurs when Moses is living in Midian and working for his father-in-law as a shepherd (Exodus 3). During that time he approaches the mountain, which in this account is called Mount Horeb, and he sees a burning bush. It is on fire, but the fire is not consuming or harming anything. This is the place and time where God appoints Moses to return to Egypt and lead the people of Israel out of their slavery. The burning bush at Mount Horeb was a dramatic sign of God's wonder and majesty, a miracle designed to inspire Moses.

Most scholars assume that "Horeb" and "Sinai" are the same mountain, although there is also some reason to think otherwise. It is entirely possible that these were two mountains close together or two peaks of the same mountain, but in the end it doesn't change the story or the meaning. In all the accounts of Horeb/Sinai, the mountain is referred to as the "Mountain of God"; that title alone clearly ties them together.

The second incident was when God gave the Ten Commandments to Moses. Moses had to climb the mountain four times over a period of several weeks, once spending forty days at the cold, bare summit. This was a time of intense instruction directly from the great Jehovah, but even during this most sacred event, there was rampant immorality in the community that remained at the base of the mountain. Apparently the nation of Israel leaned on Moses rather than God; they found their strength and confidence in him rather than in the God he represented. It is a lesson for us, lest we think that our spiritual well-being requires the ministry of any one person.

During this time, the "Mountain of God" is described as being covered in smoke and fire and actually "trembling"; the great mountain of Sinai shook. Some have opined that this is evidence of a volcano, but that view seems to diminish the grandeur of God, in whose presence smoke and fire and shaking mountains are easily understandable as the Almighty makes contact with the mortal. Surely it is not too difficult to see that smoke and fire are appropriate for the appearance of God and that anything is likely to tremble when the great Jehovah is personally present (galaxies, let alone mountains). You decide about that, but be clear that whatever happened was by the immediate and personal touch of God and not the result of some mindless, natural process.

The third incident on Mount Horeb, "the Mountain of God," occurred when Elijah was running in fear from King Ahab and Queen Jezebel—that royal Bonnie and Clyde—after he had humiliated the prophets of Baal. When he reached that sacred mountain, discouraged and afraid, he was arrested by the presence of God, reassured of his vital ministry and instructed to return and anoint Elisha as his successor.

In each case, the mountain was a place of godly instruction, and in the one case, it was the site where God delivered the Law that He intended to govern all human affairs and which even today is the foundation of many of the world's legal systems.

> Earth's crammed with heaven
>
> And every common bush afire with God;
>
> But only he who sees takes off his shoes.
>
> —Elizabeth Barrett Browning

> *Now Moses was tending the flock of Jethro his father-in-law, the priest of Midian, and he led the flock to the far side of the desert and came to Horeb, the mountain of God. There the angel of the Lord appeared to him in flames of fire from within a bush.*
>
> Exodus 3:1–2a

Moses had grown up in the Egyptian royal court after being adopted by the princess, but as an adult he committed murder and had to flee for his life. That flight took him to Midian, far away from metropolitan Egypt both in culture and distance. In Midian, the former princeling married a local woman and became a common shepherd among a desert tribe. It was a long fall from grace, but there is no suggestion that Moses complained or grumbled. He spent the next forty years humbly tending the flocks of his father-in-law. It was surely a dramatic change of lifestyle for one who grew up in Pharaoh's palace.

And things were no better for the Israelites in Egypt. While Moses adjusted to the life of a poor sheep tender in the desert, his beloved people in Egypt *groaned in their slavery* under the harsh rule of their Egyptian masters. They were all miserable and God heard those groans, and initiated the process that would deliver them out of bondage. He appeared to Moses in a burning bush and sent him back to Egypt as their leader and deliverer. But during this memorable burning-bush event in the desert, there are two noteworthy statements by God.

First, He tells Moses, *"Take off your sandals, for the place where you are standing is holy ground"* (Exodus 3:5). And that begs the question of just what makes that ground holy. It was not holy because of its beauty or its history or its worldly importance. It was holy because God had set apart that patch of desert to be used for His purposes, and on that basis alone it was "holy." It is a reminder for us that He calls us to be dedicated (set apart) and consecrated for His purposes; that we are called to be holy.

In the United Kingdom, official mail is franked with the letters O.H.M.S. That is an abbreviation for On His (or Her) Majesty's Service. It is mail that has been set apart for special handling and devoted purposes. In a similar way, the burning bush—and our lives—carry that stamp "O.H.M.S." because both are intended for royal purposes. It and we are holy ground because it and we have been selected for royal service.

Second, during this encounter, Moses asks God who he should say has sent him. Surely the Israelites will ask of Moses who it is that he thinks has given him this extraordinary authority and responsibility. Who is this being? And Moses is instructed to tell them that he has been sent by "I AM." God elaborates that He is *the Lord, the God of your fathers—the God of Abraham, the God of Isaac and the God of Jacob"* (Exodus 3:15), but He then reiterates that the name He wants to be known by and to be remembered by is I AM. The fundamental meaning of this Hebrew word is something like "to exist." God is saying to Moses that he can tell the Israelites that the one who has authorized and sent him is the one who simply is I AM.

It is an enigmatic title, but it conveys the sense that God is more than an impersonal force and that He is the foundation of everything else. He is not the one who became or the one who developed or the one who evolved. He is the one who simply exists and has always existed and will always exist. He is in the simplest possible grammar, I AM. At a later time, Jesus would describe Himself in the same terms when he told the Pharisees, *"I tell you the truth before Abraham was born, I am!"* (John 8:58), leaving those religious hypocrites to ponder the meaning.

It is a stark contrast with human attempts at importance. Important men and women have often desired to be known as rich, talented, famous, or powerful. They love to be addressed as "president," "senator," or "captain." But generals and bishops and governors eventually die and return to dust. Their titles and accolades slowly evaporate in the natural process of history. God, on the other hand, desires only to be known as I AM.

Take the Ten Commandments, for example. People joke about them, do they not?

They even make films of them.

They do everything but keep them.

—Martyn Lloyd-Jones

When the Lord finished speaking to Moses on Mount Sinai, he gave him the two tablets of the Testimony, the tablets of stone inscribed by the finger of God.

Exodus 31:18

Mount Horeb Sinai

So on this mountain God gave to mankind a list of behaviors that constituted His standard for appropriate, holy living. These were not ten suggestions; they were ten mandates, ten decrees. These were laws to be observed and they were laws ordered directly from God, the I AM God. There was and is no room for compromise or revision. They were written in stone for a purpose.

Ever since Sinai, there has been a history of attempts to undermine those laws. The Jews found them to be too restrictive and went on to worship multiple other gods. Other cultures simply ignored them at their will or adopted them as secular laws when that was helpful. God's clarity and focus in these ten laws quickly became blurred and remains so today because men and women fail to understand their greatness and holiness. In my hometown, a wonderful and godly judge had a copy of those ten laws posted in his courtroom since they are—indeed— the foundation of all Western law. But other courts, including the US Supreme Court, ordered that they be removed lest they might in some unexplained way be "offensive" to somebody. Today they still hang in that courtroom, although covered by a sheet. But they still hang there and function as an unseen spiritual basis for his judicial decisions.

Chuck Colson was invited to speak at a public high school on one occasion, and when he visited with the principal in his office, he was told that there were no copies of the Ten Commandments posted in the school because that was against their policy. Before the speech, he was given a tour by that same principal. As they walked the main hallway, past the rows of student lockers, the principal mentioned that students were required to have a lock on their lockers because there was a serious problem of theft. Anything in an unlocked locker would likely be stolen. In a moment of reflection, the principal asked Chuck Colson if he had any suggestions about how to deal with the problem and Chuck quickly replied, "You could always post a sign that says, *'Thou shalt not steal.'*"

Oh, *And thou shall have no other gods, and thou shall honor thy mother and father, and thou shall not lie (bear false witness), and thou shall not commit adultery,* etc. (Exodus 20:2–17).

The Ten Commandments were and are holy, directly from God, intended for our good, and perfectly formulated as holy, holy, holy. They were first handed to humankind on Mount Sinai through the person of Moses, in a scene of great reverence and majesty. But the commandments themselves are no less majestic and splendid in their design and their purpose than they were when the stone tablets were still electric with the touch of God.

Further, the Ten Commandments were not the last decrees that God delivered to us. The New Testament is filled with instructions that are not labeled as commandments but are given without any reservation. In every case, they are given in the imperative mood, which is the linguistic method of issuing an order. "Do your homework!" is imperative. *Add to your faith* in 2 Peter 1:5 is imperative and it is followed by the specifics to be added: *goodness, knowledge, self-control, perseverance, godliness, brotherly kindness, and love.* In addition, *clothe yourself* in Colossians 3:12 is imperative and is followed by the objects to be put on: *compassion, kindness, humility, gentleness, and patience.*

As you read through both testaments, you will encounter many imperatives (commands) and it is clear that these carry the same force of authority as the Ten Commandments. The issues may not be as momentous, but all of these imperatives are direct, clear, and without qualifications or conditions. They are commands from the heart of God.

But, don't stop here.

Obedience is the fruit of faith.

—Christina Rossetti

This is how we know that we love the children of God: by loving God
and carrying out his commands. This is love for God: to obey his
commands. And his commands are not burdensome.

1 John 5:2–3

Sinai was the location that God chose to deliver His great com-mandments to His people through Moses. Through the succeeding centuries, it became abundantly clear that this perfect and holy "Law" did little more than expose the moral imperfection of humankind. Over and over again, God's holy Law was trashed by the behavior of men and women. Its ultimate purpose was to expose that corrupt human nature. The Law was perfect, and humanity was not, so they were in that sense incompatible but mutually revealing.

God's merciful, gracious, and ingenious solution to this problem was to send His Son, Jesus, to pay the price for our sins. The Law was impeccable in every way, but humanity was not. Because of that moral flaw, a Savior was needed to deliver humankind from the guilt and penalty of those transgressions (sins). That Savior was Jesus and He paid the price for all the sins of all those who would believe that simple fact by faith.

So, under the New Testament, God's instruction is to write the Law on our hearts. That is His point of concern. Thus we are not hammered for every infraction since Jesus has delivered us from the law of sin and death (Romans 8:2).

So this leads to a new understanding of the word *obedience*. And while God is still God and He is still concerned that we remain faithful to His Law, the kind of obedience He desires under this new covenant is something like a law of agreement. Think about this . . .

If the I AM is who He claims to be, then His Law can be nothing else than perfect—perfect in its formation and perfect in its benefits. If the Law is perfect, then we would be truly foolish to ignore or defy it. If the Law is really perfect in its content and its results, it would be only logical to agree with it so that our resultant behavior would be something more like concession or assent to the obvious than simple and rigid obedience.

Interstate speeding laws are not always perfect and so our obedience is based on raw discipline and conformity. Tax laws are often oppressive, but we obey them for fear of penalty. The great Law of the I AM is perfect and holy and just and beneficial, and as we grasp that truth, our compliance with those laws will be out of a sense of agreement rather than simple duty.

Mount Sinai was the location where that great Law was handed directly from God to humanity. It is the geographical location where God reached out with a written copy of His perfect Law for our welfare and protection. It is the mountain of godly instruction and godly Law directly from the I AM.

> The sheer brilliance of the Ten Commandments is that they codify, in a handful of words, acceptable behavior. Not just for then or now but for all time.
>
> —Ted Koppel

> *Hear, O Israel: The Lord our God, the Lord is one.*
> *Love the Lord your God with all your heart and with all your soul*
> *and with all your strength. These commandments that I give you*
> *today are to be upon your hearts. Impress them on your children.*
> *Talk about them when you sit at home and when you walk along the*
> *road, when you lie down and when you get up.*
>
> Deuteronomy 6:4–7

CHAPTER FIVE

EBAL: MOUNTAIN OF REMINDER

Remember how far you have come,
not just how far you have to go.

—Rick Warren

*When you have crossed the Jordan into the land the Lord your God
is giving you, set up some large stones and coat them with plaster.
Write on them all the words of this law . . . and . . . set up these stones
on Mount Ebal. . . . And you shall write very clearly all the words of
this law on these stones you have set up.*

Deuteronomy 27:2–4, 8

MOUNT EBAL STANDS IN THE area now referred to as the West
Bank, an area inhabited since 1948 by Palestinians. That area was once
a part of Israel and formed an important landmark for the Jews as
they travelled from their captivity in Egypt and entered the land of
Canaan. Ebal rises to 3,109 feet above sea level and forms the north
side of the Shechem pass opposite Mount Gerizim. From the summit
of Ebal, the skyline of Tel Aviv is clearly visible. Ebal is a pronounced
geologic landmark and the site of a significant event in the history
of the Jewish people.

Mount Ebal marked the first and most prominent landmark for
the nation of Israel when they began to occupy the promised land of

Canaan. They had come a long way, both in miles and in time. The entire nation of Israel had walked hundreds of miles through barren desert over a period of forty years. An entire generation had passed away during that pilgrimage. Great tragedies had afflicted them in the form of disease and hunger, earthquakes and poisonous snakes, ruthless enemies and spiritual apathy, but they had finally arrived at the place God had chosen for them. A place of abundance and permanence where they could at last settle, build a protected country, and enjoy rest from those years of uncertainty and anxiety. They were, in a very real sense, home, even though they had never been there before. They were finally at the destination they had longed for. And their great leader, Joshua, had one final task before he died at the rich age of 110.

None of this was a surprise because God had commanded it through Moses many years before. The Great Jehovah (just another labored translation of the enigmatic Hebrew word for I AM) had delivered a command through Moses to stop at the very entrance to the Promised Land, at a place called Mount Ebal, and erect an altar of uncut stones on which they were to write *all the words of this law* (Deuteronomy 27:4) as a memorial and a point of remembrance. It was a pivotal event because it was intended to be a monumental reminder of how far they had come, of the great God who had guided and protected them, and of His holy and perfect Law as their standard of living.

Mount Ebal was God's choice of a place for remembering His goodness and greatness. Mount Ebal is a symbol of the value of remembering both how far we have come and how far we have to go.

> My memory is nearly gone; but I remember two things;
> that I am a great sinner, and that Christ is a great Savior.
>
> —John Newton

On my bed I remember you;

I think of you through the watches of the night.

Because you are my help,

I sing in the shadow of your wings.

Psalm 63:6–7

Everyone complains about their memory. Children have endless excuses for not remembering their homework or their chores or to brush their teeth. Parents forget appointments and passwords and where they left the car keys. Surgeons forget to remove implements after surgery. Shoppers forget where they parked their car. Everyone struggles with memory. And God knew that and commanded several times in Scripture to remember key events and to create objects that would stimulate those memories.

At one time, I worked with a man who had a truly phenomenal memory. He could listen to someone read off the playing cards from a full deck that had been thoroughly shuffled and then recite them frontwards or backwards, or for any named card he could remember which cards were immediately before or after it. I don't know if he could remember where his car was in the parking lot, but I do know he could perform incredible feats of short-term memory.

On the other hand, I have another friend who claims, "I remember exactly where I put everything. But, when I look for it, it's not there."

By contrast, God is not interested in short-term memory; He is interested in the long view. The aging John Newton (author of the hymn "Amazing Grace") remembered two crucial, long-term things. He remembered the two things that are so long term that they stretch backward to our spiritual birth and forward to eternity. He remembered that he was, by nature, a great sinner and that a great Savior had saved him for eternity. It is the long term that counts.

Those two elements join at the cross and form the one great issue that needs constant remembrance. It is dangerously easy for us to forget that our basic nature is not nice; that we are powerfully motivated to please ourselves first, that we do not naturally choose the desires and wishes of God and others over our own.

It is easy to forget that we are proud, impatient, insensitive, envious, and greedy. We are not nice people by birth, but we can become quite nice by remembering our inherent character and allowing the Spirit of God to move us in other and better directions. When I remember that I am a great sinner, I remember to do something about it, beginning with enlisting the potent help of the Holy Spirit. However, when I forget that fatal flaw and push ahead with my natural, sinful motivations, other people are hurt and I am diminished.

It is also surprisingly easy to forget the work of atonement accomplished by Jesus Christ on the cross. When that is forgotten, Jesus becomes a pale, shallow preacher of platitudes that seem disconnected and somewhat irrelevant. There is no more powerful or motivating remembrance than the fact that Jesus Christ lived and died and rose again in order to be our Great Savior.

Joshua erected an altar of stone on Mount Ebal so the nation of Israel would remember the goodness and greatness of God. I forget those too, and for that reason, on the banks of the Chickenboro Brook in the Waterville Valley of New Hampshire, not far from the viaduct under Goose Hollow Road, there is a great boulder with a cross chiseled into the surface that I carved there purposely on August 9, 1979, to remind me of those great facts. We all need reminders.

We need reminders because we so easily forget. It is the significance of Mount Ebal, mountain of remembrance.

> Christian, remember the goodness of God in the frost of adversity.
>
> —Charles Spurgeon

Many, O Lord my God,

are the wonders you have done.

The things you planned for us

no one can recount to you;

were I to speak and tell of them,

they would be too many to declare.

Psalm 40:5

It is good also to remember the many blessings of the past, especially when we are confronted with present troubles. It is good to remember those blessings at all times because they are a reminder of God's compassion and mercy and grace.

Very early in our history, God created the rainbow so that we would be reminded of His covenant to never again destroy the world by means of a flood. The elegance of a rainbow is our reminder of His goodness to Noah and through Noah to us all.

Moses went to great effort to make sure that the wandering nation of Israel did not forget God's deliverance from the oppression of Egypt and the parting of the Red Sea, the ten miraculous plagues that preceded that deliverance, the great and dramatic days of receiving God's commandments, God's care for them in the desert with food and water, God's mercy and grace in response to their unfaithfulness, and God's punishment of disobedience and rebellion. The book of Deuteronomy is filled with challenges to remember the goodness of God.

Jesus' mother, Mary, was one who exercised her memory of God's goodness. She was an active participant in the incarnation of God as a fragile infant and the apostle Luke takes time to tell us that *she treasured up all these things and pondered them in her heart.* She remembered that birth night and the angels and the music and the simple shepherds and the entire experience because it was such a magnificent display of God's goodness. Later, when Jesus was twelve and they all traveled to Jerusalem, Jesus lagged behind to discuss eternal issues with the temple teachers so that Mary and Joseph had to return and find him. Again it says that the experience was so meaningful and lovely that Mary treasured all these things in her heart.

So, what is there in our lives that should be treasured, stored, and remembered? The moment of our salvation when we recognized with clear assurance that we were loved by God and our sins were healed by His sacrifice? Recovery from an acute illness? Rescue from danger? Provision in a time of critical need? Spiritual comfort at a moment of stress or grief or fear? Gracious answer to a prayer that seemed futile? Healing of a child, a parent, a sibling, or a spouse? A painful trial that you now recognize as the instructive hand of God?

And what reminders have we erected? A diary of memories? Notes in our Bible? Some physical object specifically intended to be our Mount Ebal stones? There is plenty of room on that rock on the banks of the Chickenboro if you care to leave your own reminder, and there are plenty of stones elsewhere. It is good to remember the goodness of God and especially in the frost of adversity.

One thing we do need to remember is that forgiven sins are buried and gone. Through the prophet Jeremiah, the Lord said, *"I will forgive their wickedness and will remember their sins no more"* (31:34). It is thoroughly normal to be disturbed by sins of our past, which we know are forgiven, theologically speaking, but which still disturb our fundamental peace with vivid memories and regrets, with guilt and shame. In those cases, there is a sort of backwards remembrance, a remembrance that we can forget those sins because God has removed them completely.

Memory discipline is the key to understanding forgiveness, both God's and ours. It is a bedrock principle. God has pronounced at least four times in Scripture that He would not remember our confessed sins (Hebrews 8:12; 10:17; Isaiah 43:25; Jeremiah 31:34). But notice that He does not ever promise to forget; instead He promises to *"not remember,"* which requires a conscious effort. It may sound like an insignificant difference, but it is not. Forgetting is akin to deleting a computer file and then moving on. But that doesn't work for forgiveness because forgiveness always involves a personal offense and those cannot be simply deleted.

God's example for us is to *"not remember,"* which implies some serious and deliberate control of any shame or guilt thoughts from personal sin that has been confessed and for which we know from Scripture God has forgiven. In *Spiritual Depression: Its Causes and Cures*, Martyn Lloyd-Jones wisely instructs us to not allow that past that God has dealt with to rob us of joy: "O let us remember that it is sin to doubt God's Word. It is sin to allow the past, which God has dealt with, to rob us of our joy and our usefulness in the present and in the future."

Conversely, in regard to grievous offenses that we have endured and then forgiven, this thought control can be time consuming and tiring, but it is God's standard and He has instructed us to do the same. The Bible says, *"Forgiving each other, just as in Christ God forgave you"* (Ephesians 4:32) and to *forgive as the Lord forgave you* (Colossians 3:13). And, His method of forgiveness is to *"not remember"*; it is to take control of our memory in a way that overrides the natural tendency to contemplate and meditate on a wrong we have suffered.

And there is further encouragement in 2 Corinthians 10:5 where Paul says to *take captive every thought to make it obedient to Christ.*

So, Joshua was commanded to set up a memorial on Mount Ebal so that the nation of Israel would always remember the multitude of God's blessings and the solemnity of His Law. It is a colorful example for us as we live through the difficulties and joys of life to remember the God who is behind them all.   *IT'S ALL ABOUT GOD*

But, in contrast to that encouragement for us to remember God's law and blessings, is the promise that God *does not* remember our sins that have been forgiven and that we should do the same.

It is an interesting contrast. Remember the one and do not remember the other. Remember the blessings and the Law because we need always to recognize the priority of God in our life. Do not remember forgiven sin because it reminds us of God's mercy and grace.

Remember these. Don't remember those.

Mount Ebal and the monument erected by Joshua are a reminder of both. We need reminders and we need them because there are critical issues to remember, and those issues have significant impact on how we live out these years of mortal life. To remember is to find motivation. And when we remember the right things, we find motivation to do the right things.

> Let us remember the loving-kindness of the Lord and rehearse His deeds of grace. Let us open the volume of recollection, which is so richly illuminated with memories of His mercy, and we will soon be happy.
>
> —Charles Haddon Spurgeon

Praise the Lord, O my soul,

and forget not all his benefits.

Psalm 103:2

Yet this I call to mind and therefore I have hope.

Because of the Lord's great love we are not consumed.

Lamentations 3:21–22a

CHAPTER SIX

GILEAD: MOUNTAIN OF COURAGE

Courage is not simply one of the virtues but the form of every virtue at the testing point, which means at the point of highest reality.

—C. S. Lewis

"Anyone who trembles with fear may turn back and leave Mount Gilead." So twenty-two thousand men left, while ten thousand remained."

Judges 7:3b

MOUNT GILEAD IS LOCATED IN present-day Jordan between the Wadi Mujib and Yarmouk River, a tributary of the Jordan that partially defines the border between Israel and the country of Jordan. The name Gilead means "rugged" and the Old Testament describes it as being heavily forested (see Jeremiah 22:6–7). Its contours are that of a long ridgeline rather than a single mountain peak, so you can picture a long ridge of about 3,000 feet in elevation, covered with cedar trees.

In Gideon's day the major trade route, the King's Highway, ran from Egypt to Damascus over that mountain and thus it was a critical choke point for commerce. If you lived in the Middle East in biblical times, you knew something about Mount Gilead.

In the story of Gideon's opposition to the Midianite invaders, Mount Gilead is a geographical point of decision for men about to be confronted with a fierce battle against an overwhelming enemy. It was on Mount Gilead that the great leader Gideon challenged his soldiers to decide and here I paraphrase Judges 7:3: *"If you are too afraid to continue; if you lack the courage for this battle; go home. We cannot win without courage and on this mountain you must declare."* At that moment, 22,000 men admitted that they did not have the courage to continue, and so they voted with their feet to avoid the battle. Ten thousand men of courage remained.

Courage is not the absence of fear, but rather the judgment that something else is more important than fear.

—Ambrose Redmoon

For God gave us a spirit not of fear but of power and love and self-control.

2 Timothy 1:7 (ESV)

The Midianites were a scourge on the land of Israel and had been from the times of Moses. This wandering tribe of desert nomads were descendants of Abraham through his second wife, Keturah. It is one more example that even the finest families can have difficult children despite their best efforts. Humankind is a fallen race, prone to sin, and our children are no different. Even with godly examples and wise teaching, some children will simply drift away into sin and rebellion.

Somewhere these descendants of Moses went bad. And they became a powerful race of animal herders who lived a nomadic existence in the desert but also invaded fertile agricultural areas every year to graze their cattle and carry off the grain and other seasonal supplies. Their destructive ravages were a serious blight on Israel's fortunes and severely threatened the very existence of that nation. That pattern is well known in some parts of the world today. In West Africa, the cattle-herding Fulani nomads are in constant conflict with the settled Bambara crop farmers as they both compete for their own interests in the land.

But this antipathy between Israel and Midian was not simply agrarian. In Moses' time, the Midianites had enticed many Israeli men and women into the worship of their abominable god Baal, and in order to restore spiritual purity, Moses had killed all of the men and most of the women and taken all of their property. These events created a long standing enmity between the two nations, but Gideon's primary concern was the economic survival of Israel in the face of rampant Midianite plunder and terror.

The Midianites are a reminder of the old demons that beset anyone. Certainly we have power in Christ to be victorious, but there are times when we must fight courageously for that victory. It was Paul himself who reminded us that we do not fight against other people but against *the powers of this dark world and against the spiritual forces of evil* (Ephesians 6:12).

Gideon's courage, based on his raw faith in the sovereign God, led to an unimaginable victory. God whittled his 32,000-man army down to 300 and those 300—by the power of God—utterly defeated countless thousands of Midianites. But then, it wasn't Gideon who defeated them; it was God Himself who had the victory, and it is always so. We can exercise courage, but it is God who wins the battle.

One man with courage makes a majority.

—Andrew Jackson

Be on your guard; stand firm in the faith; be men of courage; be strong. Do everything in love.

1 Corinthians 16:13–14

Any Christian's spiritual life requires courage, because we live in a fallen world where current-day "Midianites" are prone to intimidate us with ridicule and sarcasm and all manner of criticism for our foolish faith, and our antiquated morality, in a world of relativism and materialism. Our modern Midianites may be family members or coworkers or friends or professors or others, but anyone considering that initial step of reconciliation with God through simple faith in the atoning work of Jesus is likely to encounter intimidation or ridicule.

The battle of Gettysburg was fought July 1–3, 1863. It produced more casualties than any other battle of the American Civil War and is often described as that war's turning point. Historians still debate the battle's significance, but they all agree that it stopped further advance by the Confederacy into the North and severely impaired that breakaway nation's ability to maintain the offensive. Further, if the Union army had failed at Gettysburg, Washington, DC, would have been exposed to attack, and it is possible that the war would have ended in favor of the South.

On the second day of the battle of Gettysburg, General George Pickett led 12,000 Confederate troops across open ground against the Union Army's positions on Cemetery Ridge. The end of that ridgeline was a small hill known as Little Roundtop, and that far left end of the Union line was manned by the 20th Maine volunteers, commanded by a former college professor who had proven his tactical skills and courage in previous battles. Colonel Joshua Chamberlain was a thirty-five-year-old citizen soldier whose courage on this day would change the course of the war.

After almost two hours of intense fighting, Colonel Chamberlain's men were nearly out of ammunition and his position was vulnerable to a flanking operation by the Confederates, which would most likely have turned the battle into a Confederate victory. That one spot and that one unit held the outcome of the battle and possibly the war.

Understanding the critical nature of their situation, Colonel Chamberlain ordered his men to fix bayonets and personally led them in a charge directly into the oncoming Confederate soldiers. At one point, a Confederate officer held a pistol within inches of Chamberlain's face and pulled the trigger, but the gun misfired and Chamberlain continued the attack. The Union soldiers were so inspired by their commander that they pressed the charge, pushed back the brave Confederates, and held the end of the line and by so doing the entire line itself.

Col. Chamberlain was awarded the Medal of Honor for his bravery in the contest. Gideon was a citizen soldier of great courage, as were his men. Joshua Chamberlain was a citizen soldier, as were his men. In both cases, those leaders knew there was something more important than fear and acted on that conviction. Similarly, those who are confronted with the gospel claims of Christ need to know there is something more important than fear, something eternally important.

In West Africa, I encountered two men who were examples of spiritual and secular courage. These two men had been raised in Muslim families and had come to faith in Christ as young men despite their clear understanding that this commitment would place their lives in jeopardy. No conversions from Islam were allowed. "Infidels" would not be tolerated. Both men knew that, but because they were also convicted of something more important than fear, they both publicly committed their lives to Christ. In each case, the mother tried to kill them with poison. One man's brother inadvertently drank the poison and died. The other survived when a relative drank the poison and that relative is now crippled for life. Today both of those men, from very different locations and backgrounds, are vibrant and courageous Christian leaders. No one knows how many others have been killed for their faith under similar circumstances. Only the survivors can be counted or heard.

In western Pakistan, I met a man who had been a Muslim mullah, a Muslim cleric and spiritual leader. One day he heard on the radio that someone was offering a correspondence course about Christianity and so he subscribed. In time, and despite fearful threats, he became a

Christ follower and eventually became a missionary to the wild tribal area known as Waziristan, an area with no law other than by village leaders who rule according to their view of Islamic principles. When I visited with him, he said he was committed to spreading the gospel in those dangerous areas because no one else would. He said that the children, especially, loved the message of Jesus and that he knew he would be killed. It was a certainty.

When I returned a year later and inquired of him, he was gone—killed for his faith. For those who believe Jesus to be the Son of God and God Himself there is a motive greater than fear.

> Courage is fear that has said its prayers.
>
> —Karle Wilson Baker

> *Therefore, if you are offering your gift at the altar and there remem-*
> *ber that your brother has something against you, leave your gift*
> *there in front of the altar. First go and be reconciled to your brother;*
> *then come and offer your gift.*
>
> Matthew 5:23–24

We commonly associate courage with physical threats, but there are few things in this life that require more courage than asking or granting forgiveness of a personal offense. There is fear in asking for forgiveness and there is often a sense of fear in granting forgiveness. And, unforgiveness or a simple lack of forgiveness may be the single greatest injury to relationships. The forgiveness issue assumes that there will be offenses—Jesus said so and life repeatedly demonstrates it. And since there will be offenses, there is abundant need for forgiveness, both asking and granting. And both need the courage that is acquired by prayer. *Forgive as the Lord forgave you,* Paul wrote to the Colossians (3:13).

The basic principle of seeking forgiveness is stated in Matthew 5 where Jesus declares this issue to be so important that we should even abort our worship—if that is what we are doing—and go directly to the one we have offended; go personally, openly, and humbly. It is a chastening experience, but if we have been wrong, there is simply no way to truly restore a relationship other than the simple act of asking forgiveness. And not some insipid statement that begins with "If I have offended you . . ." or some suffix that begins with "but . . ." If you are motivated to ask for forgiveness, there is no "if" and there is no "but." You already know you have offended and because of that offense, any forgiveness demands a clear acknowledgment of the offense, followed by a request for forgiveness.

It is extremely simple to understand but very difficult to do because it is always hard to deny one's ego and act with genuine humility. Even if the other party has offended you in some grievous way, you are nevertheless responsible for your transgression. If they never reciprocate, that is not your responsibility. For this event, you will certainly need grace and humility and the "courage that is fear that has said its prayers."

Further, Paul (God, actually) commands (more than once) that we forgive whatever sins have been committed against us. There is no wiggle room in this. The commands are very direct and clear. We must not live with a broken relationship over some offense that has been committed. It must be resolved and not just ignored.

This is an act that demands great courage. It required so much of Jesus to forgive our sins that He sweat blood at the thought of the price that must be paid. Forgiveness is often difficult in the extreme and demanding of great personal courage. And yet, forgiveness is so close to God's heart that we are never more like Him or more pleasing to Him than when we forgive.

The alternative is stubborn unforgiveness. The alternative is to conclude that we have been so offended that we will respond by never giving the offending party the satisfaction of receiving our forgiveness. We will hurt him or her with our bitter and angry attitude and withhold any sense of resolution and do all this as a form of retribution. It will be the way that we get even. That will show them!

There are two problems with this attitude. First, it directly contradicts one of God's unmistakable commands for all believers. It is an ugly refusal to obey the one who has loved us and forgiven us and adopted us. Second, in a purely practical sense it just doesn't work. Unforgiveness is like drinking poison and expecting your enemy to die. It doesn't work. It backfires. We end up as the injured party. Unforgiveness is a cancer.

Forgiveness is a serious element of any Christian's life. Because life is filled with offenses, you will need to forgive and you will need forgiveness. But in order to do either one you will need the "courage that is fear that has said its prayers."

> It takes as much courage to have tried and failed as it does to have tried and succeeded.
>
> —Anne Morrow Lindbergh

> *"Be strong and courageous. Do not be terrified; do not be discouraged, for the Lord your God will be with you wherever you go."*
>
> Joshua 1:9b

Living out the Christian life requires courage because it requires faith. Jesus told His early disciples to take courage in the middle of the night in the middle of the storm in the middle of the Sea of Galilee. He didn't suggest that they suck it up and "dig deep" for that courage. He reminded them that He was there. That was enough. *"Take courage! It is I. Don't be afraid"* (Matthew 14:27).

When God intervened into Gideon's life, He asked a simple farmer and shepherd with no military training to just walk in faith as God's instrument to defeat a formidable enemy. Gideon demonstrated his faith by his courage.

And nothing has changed. God intervenes in our lives on a daily basis asking for courage that is grounded in faith. There are Gileads ahead in every life, and for those we need the example of Gideon. For those we need to know that in the midst of the battle it is God Himself who protects us.

> The first step of courage isn't taken in the midst of battle; it's taken when you're willing to walk onto the battlefield and face the unknown.
>
> —Steven Curtis Chapman

But Christ is faithful as a son over God's house. And we are his house, if we hold on to our courage and the hope of which we boast.

Hebrews 3:6

ASK FOR

COURAGE IS THAT IS GROUNDED IN FAITH

FAITH

CHAPTER SEVEN

CARMEL: MOUNTAIN OF VICTORY

When I think of death, it is in the hope of pressing, one day, some hard-fought and well-won field of battle, and dying with the shout of victory in my ear. That would be worth dying for, and more, it would be worth living for.

—Sir Walter Scott

Then the fire of the Lord fell and burned up the sacrifice, the wood, the stones and the soil, and also licked up the water in the trench. When all the people saw this, they fell prostrate and cried, "The Lord—he is God!"

1 Kings 18:38–39a

ELIJAH WITNESSED A GREAT VICTORY on Mount Carmel when God personally intervened to humiliate and defeat the priests of Baal, a vile and cruel idol of the Levantine people. At that moment, Mount Carmel became a symbol of great spiritual victory and it remains so today. Elijah on Mount Carmel is a poster child for spiritual victory.

Mount Carmel is a coastal mountain range in northern Israel stretching from the Mediterranean Sea towards the southeast. The title "Mount Carmel" has been used to refer to the entire range, or select northern parts of that range, but for these purposes we can simply imagine a mountain ridge in northern Israel rising to a modest 1,700 feet above sea level. Carmel has had a powerful influence on migrations and wars because of its strategic location and layout. It has also been known as a sacred place all through recorded history. The Egyptian pharaoh Thutmose III appears to refer to it in his account of a sacred location in what was then Canaan, 1,500 years before Christ (at least 900 years before Elijah).

It is a place rich in history. Elisha the prophet sought refuge there. King Saul erected a monument to himself there (never a good idea). David's second wife came from Carmel. Solomon used Carmel as a metaphor of a royal crown in his Song of Songs. It was a stronghold of the Essenes, a Jewish sect that retreated from the compromised religion of late Israel. In World War I the British general Allenby led his men to victory over the Turks at one of Carmel's passes in the Battle of Megiddo, and that event marked a turning point in the decline of the Ottoman Empire. This was a momentous piece of geography throughout the history of that area and continues so today as a strategic location for modern Israel's self-defense.

But the most memorable moment in the history of Carmel occurred in the ninth century before Christ at a pivotal time in Israel's history when paganism threatened the continuation of godly worship. On this mountain, the prophet Elijah found his *hard-fought and well-won field of battle* when he opposed the evil King Ahab and the apostate religious establishment in a make-or-break face-off. That event concluded with a memorable victory by the direct hand of God. It is quite a story.

> Victorious warriors win first and then go to war, while defeated warriors go to war first and then seek to win.
>
> —Sun Tzu

But you give us victory over our enemies; you put our adversaries to shame.

Psalm 44:7

Ahab was the eighth king of Israel, the northern kingdom after the breakup following the death of Solomon. Ahab was a vile man: cunning, devious, merciless, cowardly, thoroughly immoral and, at the same time, too spineless to contradict his even more evil wife, Jezebel. He was a depraved man, dominated by his pagan wife. First Kings 16:30–33 says,

> *Ahab son of Omri did more evil in the eyes of the Lord than any of those before him. He not only considered it trivial to commit the sins of Jeroboam son of Nebat, but he also married Jezebel daughter of Ethbaal king of the Sidonians, and began to serve Baal and worship him. He set up an altar for Baal in the temple of Baal that he built in Samaria. Ahab also made an Asherah pole and did more to provoke the Lord, the God of Israel, to anger than did all the kings of Israel before him.*

This "Baal" was a god of fertility, an idol who was worshiped for his supposed ability to bestow fertility on all growing things, and the worship of Baal often included open sexuality as a means of honoring Baal's purpose. As the god of fertility, Baal was also the god of rain and thunder, since water was required for bountiful crops.

Asherah was a female goddess, sometimes considered to be Baal's consort, likewise connected with fertility and also worshiped in perverse sexual ways. Temples to these gods housed temple prostitutes—both male and female—and engaging those prostitutes in sexual activity was considered a form of worship.

This was the setting for Elijah's ministry. He was a man, called of God, to speak out against the idolatry and evil of this ruthless, royal couple and their grotesque idolatry. Ahab and Jezebel held all the civil and religious authority in their hands. They were the law. They could do whatever they wanted with Elijah or anyone else, including systematic assassination of Jewish prophets, and others.

Against this backdrop, Elijah confronted Ahab for his wickedness and proclaimed that there would be no rain until Elijah said there would be rain. It was a direct challenge to Ahab, and Ahab's confidence in that idol god Baal, who was supposed to be in control of the weather. Elijah then went into hiding and for three years there was a devastating drought.

After three years, Elijah emerged and challenged Ahab by suggesting a face-off between Elijah and his God, and the priests/prophets of Baal and their god. It was time for a direct confrontation between good and evil, between truth and deception, between God and idols.

Elijah suggested that each side be given a bull, that the bulls be slaughtered and the pieces laid on separate altars on Mount Carmel. Then the priests of Baal and Elijah, in turn, would call on their god/God to send down fire to consume this sacrifice.

The priests of Baal prepared their bull and 450 of them called on their idol god from morning until noon. They cut themselves with swords and lances and danced in a frenzy around their altar, calling for Baal to send fire. But it never came. *No one came; no one paid attention* (1 Kings 18:29). It must have been quite a spectacle. Four hundred fifty whirling, frantic pagan priests crying and begging their stone god for a sign, cutting themselves and streaming blood, and all for nothing.

Then it was Elijah's turn. One man of God under the scrutiny of 450 pagan priests and the king. Elijah cut up his bull and laid it on the altar. Then he had his helpers bring large jars of water to pour over the sacrifice and the altar. They did this until the sacrifice was soaked and the water filled the trench that was dug around the altar base.

When all this had been done, Elijah prayed that God would show His power and authority by sending fire to consume the sacrifice; and the fire came. It consumed the bull and the wood and the water and the stones and the dust and the water in the trench. And all the people fell on their faces and said, *"The Lord, He is God"* (1 Kings 18:39). And the people seized all the prophets of Baal and killed them.

It was a marvelous victory. The great, holy, majestic, powerful God of heaven demonstrated His power in a very tangible way and utterly exposed the emptiness and impotence of pagan gods.

But you give us victory over our enemies,

you put our adversaries to shame.

Psalm 44:7

Incidentally, Ahab died in battle and dogs ate his blood. And Jezebel was thrown from a window and horses trampled her body until only her skull and hands remained. God's adversaries were openly put to shame.

> God is the Champion at bringing people from a place of destruction to a place of total victory. As they reach that place of victory they become trophies of his grace; and they are set on display as a fragrant reminder of God's goodness.
>
> —Joyce Meyer

But thanks be to God, who always leads us in triumphal procession in Christ and through us spreads everywhere the fragrance of the knowledge of him.

For we are to God the aroma of Christ among those who are being saved and those who are perishing.

To the one we are the smell of death; to the other, the fragrance of life. And who is equal to such a task?

2 Corinthians 2:14–16

I suggest that you read this short passage from 2 Corinthians again because it is pregnant with meaning, and meaning that is related to victory.

Paul is describing a Roman "triumph" in this passage and using that event to make his point. In order to get the full idea, it is important to understand what that affair was (although first-century Roman citizens would know immediately what Paul was referring to).

First, understand that Roman legions were not allowed in Rome. It was a measure designed to prevent a military coup. No large units of the Roman army could march through or camp in Rome, ever, except . . .

When a Roman general had a particularly dramatic victory over an enemy of the state, he could formally request a *"triumphus"* from the senate.

This "triumph" was a festive procession of his victorious army through the streets of Rome without arms but as a public celebration of their great victory, comparable to our ticker tape parades in major cities of America. It was a great procession with the victorious general at the lead in a gilded chariot while someone held a laurel wreath over his head. It was customary for the general to conduct himself with apparent humility even though he was dressed in red and gold garments that reminded the people of a deity.

Behind the general was the army, radiant in dress uniforms, scarlet capes, and polished helmets, marching with Roman vigor and precision. And behind the army were the captives of war in rags and chains, limping their way towards their execution. And over all of this was a cloud of incense from the many temples and shrines that covered the capital city.

Now, if you can visualize that procession, and imagine the pervasive aroma of burning incense, you can see that the meaning of that aroma depends on the situation of each individual. If you are a member of the triumphant Roman army, that aroma is the joyful smell of victory and glory and reward and you will always associate it with that. If you are one of the captives in chains, the smell of incense will be the smell of impending death because that is where you are headed. *To the one we are the smell of death; to the other, the fragrance of life* (2 Corinthians 2:16).

Paul is making a metaphor out of all this by saying that we all are marching through life in a great triumphal procession with Jesus Christ leading the parade. Everyone is marching in that parade regardless of their spiritual condition. It is a universal parade.

We who believe in Jesus Christ by faith and declare Him to be our Lord are like that incense in our influence on the world. We who believe in Christ are like a sweet fragrance in the parade of life because we have the opportunity to spread compassion, kindness, gentleness, humility, patience, brotherly kindness, and love in a world generally given to pride, cruelty, racism, greed, and more.

Christians who live out a victorious life in the midst of the world's turmoil are a fragrant reminder that there is eternal life. According to Hebrews 9:27, *it is appointed to man once to die and then the judgment.*

To those who are saved we are the fragrance of life and to those who are not we are the smell of death. It is a vivid image of victory and defeat; Jesus as the victorious general leading His splendid army in the triumphal procession while those who have rejected the truth are straggling behind to eternal defeat. The aroma is the same for all, but its meaning is starkly different.

> I count him braver who overcomes his desires than him who conquers his enemies, for the hardest victory is over self.
>
> —Aristotle

> *For everyone born of God overcomes the world. This is the victory that has overcome the world, even our faith.*
>
> 1 John 5:4

If we would march in the triumph with the victors, we must first join the army. Civilians and bystanders did not share in the honors. In God's economy it is not possible to be a victor without faith any more than a Roman soldier could be a Roman soldier without allegiance to the emperor. If you want to reserve a place for yourself in the victory section of the parade, you must do so with faith, because *this is the victory that has overcome the world, even our faith* (1 John 5:4). Those without faith bring up the rear. They smell the same aroma, but it is a reminder of an unpleasant end.

But those who join the faith army are expected to act like soldiers. It is a different kind of army. You cannot join on the basis of your talent or strength or intelligence. You can join this army only by faith and once in, you demonstrate your military status by your behavior and your strength is a gift from God. Those virtues listed above are the behavioral fruits that certify your status as a soldier in Jesus' army. They won't get you in, but they will testify to the fact that you belong. And each virtue is an opportunity to win victories because each one is an opportunity to do battle for us who live by faith but nevertheless retain a decadent nature.

Elijah presided over a great victory on Mount Carmel. It was a great victory because he was vastly outnumbered and still succeeded. He was a man of great faith, but it would be a mistake to see Elijah's faith from this side of the event as if the outcome was known with certainty. Elijah did not know how this would turn out. He knew that God was God and Baal was not, but he nevertheless was forced to move ahead one step at a time by faith, and when he did he was able to participate in a great victory.

And such are we. *With God we will gain the victory, and he will trample down our enemies* (Psalm 60:12). There is no certainty to anything in this life, but we know that God is God, that He is always up to something good, and that we can move ahead in increments by faith. And we know that as we do, we are an aroma to the world around us.

In *Grace for the Moment*, Max Lucado wrote, "When God looks at you, he doesn't see you; he sees the One who surrounds you. That means that failure is not a concern for you. Your victory is secure."

> The reason why many fail in battle is because they wait until the hour of battle. The reason why others succeed is because they have gained their victory on their knees long before the battle came . . . Anticipate your battles; fight them on your knees before temptation comes and you will have the victory.
>
> —Reuben Archer Tory

But thanks be to God! He gives us the victory through our Lord Jesus Christ.

1 Corinthians 15:57

CHAPTER EIGHT

GILBOA: MOUNTAIN 1630
OF BITTERNESS

Hurt leads to bitterness, bitterness to anger;
travel too far that road and the way is lost.

—Terry Brooks

The next day, when the Philistines came to strip the dead, they found
Saul and his three sons fallen on Mount Gilboa.

1 Samuel 31:8

MOUNT GILBOA RISES TO THE modest elevation of 1,630 feet. It over-
looks the Jezreel Valley, an inland valley south and east of the Sea of
Galilee. Mount Gilboa is unique in the number of bitter events that
have occurred there and which are prophesied to occur in the future.
In that sense it is a mountain of bitterness. Consider . . .

The nearby valley was the scene of many bloody atrocities committed by Ahab and Jezebel, and it was the location of Jezebel's gruesome
end in which she was thrown from a window, trampled by horses,
leaving her blood spattered on the wall, and then eaten by dogs which
left only her skull, her feet and her hands.

One part of this same valley, the area of Megiddo, will be the
scene of the final battle between good and evil as described in the

New Testament book of Revelation. It will be a place of rancorous bloodshed on an unprecedented scale.

Mount Gilboa was also the site of a tragic battle between the Philistines and the armies of King Saul. The fighting was intense, and the Philistines killed Saul's sons Jonathan, Abinadab, and Malki-Shua. Then the attack focused on Saul himself and he was grievously wounded. Saul did not want to be captured and humiliated by his enemies so he fell on his own sword and died. The next day, the Philistines found Saul's body, cut off his head, and nailed his body to the wall of a nearby city. It was a pitiful ending for a confused man and his family . . . and all of Israel.

When David heard of this nasty defeat, he composed a lament for Saul and his sons and ordered that it be taught to the men of Judah:

> *"O mountains of Gilboa,*
> *may you have neither dew nor rain,*
> *nor fields that yield offerings of grain.*
> *For there the shield of the mighty was defiled,*
> *the shield of Saul. . . .*
>
> *"O daughters of Israel,*
> *weep for Saul. . . .*
>
> *"I grieve for you, Jonathan my brother;*
> *you were very dear to me. . . .*
>
> *"How the mighty have fallen!*
> *The weapons of war have perished!"*

2 Samuel 1:21, 24, 26–27

It was a moment of monumental sorrow for the entire nation. Their very first king was dead and humiliated. And his sons, his heirs, were dead. It is difficult to grasp the grief of that entire nation. And it all happened on Mount Gilboa, the mountain of bitterness.

Bitterness is like cancer.

It eats upon the host.

—Maya Angelou

See to it that no one misses the grace of God and that no bitter root
grows up to cause trouble and defile many.

Hebrews 12:15

Bitterness is a topic that occurs often in the Bible and in life as well. It is a painful and difficult response to disappointment or hurt and one that is intensely self-destructive. It is so common and so damaging that the American Psychiatric Association has debated its inclusion as a defined mental illness in the *Diagnostic and Statistical Manual of Mental Disorders* with the official name of "post-traumatic embitterment disorder." Of course, psychiatrists have a vested interest in anointing as many common behaviors as possible with the clinical label of "mental disorder" in order to justify their billing of insurance companies. They have already defined childhood rebellion as "oppositional defiance disorder" and "social anxiety" (shyness) as a sickness, along with hundreds of pages of common behaviors that are now categorized as mental illness and therefore eligible for medication and billing. Bitterness is not currently listed as an illness, but look for it soon. The point is that professional counselors are encountering so many bitter people that they are motivated to label that condition with the coveted and profitable title of "illness" or "disorder."

There is a lot of bitterness. It has always been so. From a biblical perspective, it is fair to say that bitterness is not a mental illness but a personally adopted attitude that God has specifically forbidden. It begins with discontent or frustration or distress, but it need never progress into bitterness, especially for those who believe in a living and loving God, a Savior who intercedes for them, and a Holy Spirit who is empowered to motivate them. Many people suffer truly ugly crises in their lives, but only some of those descend into that selfish and destructive attitude of bitterness.

On one occasion, David returned from battle to his hometown of Ziklag to find it destroyed, his home burned down and looted, and his wife and children kidnapped. As if that wasn't enough grief, David's men openly discussed killing him. It was a moment of monumental loss for David, but the Bible record says, *But David found strength in the Lord his God* (1 Samuel 30:6b).

I have a friend whose wonderful son was cruelly murdered in a gruesome and horrible way, but that friend and his wife have consistently sought the mercy of God and the prayers of friends, and have avoided any bitterness over an experience that would certainly qualify as the basis for great acrimony and resentment.

Bitterness is a chosen response that is both painful and destructive. It is like a spreading weed that ruins a garden, but it can be pulled out without the assistance of a medical doctor, medication, or psychological counseling. It is an attitude, and attitudes are something we can control. It may not be easy, but many things we control are not easy. And we Christ followers have the inner strength of the Holy Spirit to empower us for just such things.   *ABILITY TO DO*

Bitterness is common in the Bible, but it is never considered to be unavoidable in the manner of sickness or accident. It is everywhere identified as an inappropriate and fully avoidable attitude—something God would call sin.

Few things are bitterer than to feel bitter.
A man's venom poisons himself
more than his victim.

—Charles Buxton

And do not grieve the Holy Spirit of God, with whom you were sealed
for the day of redemption. Get rid of all bitterness.

Ephesians 4:30–31a

Bitterness is the very opposite of humility and forgiveness. It is
a deeply selfish attitude that recognizes only the intensity of one's
personal hurt but is blind to the larger vision of a personal God, of
His instruction and care and wisdom. Bitterness is the result of tunnel
vision with my cherished and tender hurt at the end of the tunnel of
unforgiveness. And it is not new.

Cain was bitter. Cain, the son of Adam, was a crop farmer. He
tilled the land and grew edible plants. His brother Abel was a shepherd,
raising animals. When they each determined to honor and worship
God in some way, Abel offered the sacrifice of an animal and Cain offered a similar sacrifice of produce. For some unexplained reason, God
preferred the animal sacrifice. He doesn't explain why, He just favors
animal sacrifice. It was an understandable disappointment for Cain, but
God spoke to him and told him bluntly to just do what was right (what
was pleasing to God) because there would always be temptations to do
otherwise and he, Cain, was responsible to master those inclinations
to do otherwise.

It was sound advice and Cain could have proceeded accordingly,
but he allowed that disappointment to draw him into bitterness.
Instead of learning from this initial worship failure and moving on
to the animal sacrifices that God preferred, Cain grew angry. And from
anger he became depressed, his depression led to bitterness, and then
out of bitterness he committed the first murder. He just bludgeoned
his brother with a rock; primitive but effective.

That first murder was the direct result of sinful self-pity and nur-
tured anger and the inevitable bitterness. It is an ugly thing, but there
is an escape and the escape is found in quiet obedience to the God
who loves us.

You are only hurting yourself with your bitterness.
For your own sake, learn from it, and then let it go.

—Rick Warren

I remember my affliction and my wandering,

the bitterness and the gall.

Lamentations 3:19

That novel you had to read in high school about Moby Dick is not really a story about a whale or a whale hunt. Rather, *Moby Dick* is a 500-page tale of human bitterness and its tragic consequences.

Ahab, captain of the whaling ship *Pequod*, prophetically bears the name of the most evil king ever to rule Israel. Ahab—the captain—had lost his leg to a whale, a white whale, in his previous voyage and now walks on an artificial stump made of whalebone. He is a man consumed by bitterness toward the whale that crippled him. It has become his life's mission to find the whale he calls "Moby Dick" to exact his revenge. More than any other thing in life, more than love or family or country or honor or spiritual comfort and truth or riches or fame, Ahab wants revenge. He is a man consumed by his bitterness.

The author describes Ahab's mental state like this: "He piled upon the whale's white hump the sum of all the general rage and hate felt by his whole race from Adam down; and then, as if his chest had been a mortar, he burst his hot heart's shell upon it."

And Ahab himself, expresses his bitterness like this:

"Thou all-destroying but unconquering whale; to the last I grapple with thee; from hell's heart I stab at thee; for hate's sake I spit my last breath at thee."

But Ahab only differs from millions of other people in the grand scope of his action. Ahab is different from your Aunt Mabel who hates men, or the bigot down the street who resents other races, but he is different only in the intensity and the scope of his bitterness. Ahab employs an entire ship and its crew to sail thousands of miles to reconcile his bitterness over a missing limb. But it is not necessary to lose a leg in order to become bitter. Any simple injury or slight or loss can initiate that progression from anger to depression to bitterness to self-destructive behavior.

In the end, Ahab finds his whale, the object of his bitterness, and he dies fastened to the whale by the very weapon of his bitterness—his harpoon—in a grisly drowning on the opposite side of the world from all that should have been his objects of love and comfort. It is a glorious symbol of the natural consequences of unconstrained bitterness.

> Bitterness is the coward's revenge on the world for having been hurt.
>
> —Zora Neale Hurston

> *For I see that you are full of*
>
> *bitterness and captive to sin.*
>
> Acts 8:23

Chapter 8 of the New Testament book of Acts includes a classic story of bitterness. It takes place in an unnamed city in Samaria. Samaria was a region in northern Israel that had developed a corrupt religious combination of Judaism and Assyrian idolatry. It was an area much given to bizarre worship and open to strange and unusual religious expressions.

In this city there was a man named Simon who had developed a considerable following by practicing some manner of sorcery. Simon promoted this sorcery and his own reputation by prodigious boasts that he was someone great. As a result, the gullible Samaritans swallowed that Kool-Aid and began to proclaim, *"This man is the divine power known as the Great Power"* (Acts 8:10).

This pattern of spiritual posturing has been used from the beginning of time and continues today. Men and women preach all forms of spiritual gibberish with great authority and style and seem to attract vast numbers of credulous people who are willing to give large amounts of money and grant considerable authority. Some cynic has said, "There is a lot of money to be made at the foot of the cross." He is right. It is shameful and disturbing but he is right.

So there was Simon, riding a crest of popularity and power based on sanctimonious magic. But then came Philip, who *preached the good news of the kingdom of God and the name of Jesus Christ, ... and they were baptized, both men and women* (Acts 8:12). Suddenly, Simon was exposed as a charlatan, and the attention shifted to Philip and the gospel of grace and mercy and salvation. Amazingly, Simon himself is converted. Simon, who has spread junk religion all over Samaria, came to see the truth of sin and salvation. Simon was so captivated that he followed Philip everywhere and was amazed at his signs and miracles. It was a beautiful thing, except . . .

When word got back to Jerusalem that a revival had started in Samaria, the apostles Peter and John were sent to Samaria to convey the Holy Spirit on some of those new believers, probably as a commissioning for public service. But in any event, Simon observed this incredible spiritual power and wanted a piece of that action. He wanted to have that same authority to deliver spiritual clout to others, so he offered the apostles money in exchange. It was a crass business deal for Simon, who had a long history of commercializing religion, but it was an ugly and sinful request to the apostles who were, at that time, the custodians of the Holy Spirit in the early church. Further, the apostles could see that Simon's request came from a sense of bitter jealousy, and they rebuked him accordingly, *"For I see that you are full of bitterness and captive to sin"* (Acts 8:23).

It was the same old pattern. Simon lost his power and prestige, and even after a personal encounter with Christ, he fostered a jealousy for that old power in a new context. He was accustomed to honor and acclaim and he wanted it back, and his jealousy led to bitterness over what had been lost. But, unlike so many others, this story has a pleasant ending. When Simon hears this chastisement from the apostles, he recognizes his sinful attitude and begs for prayer that he will be delivered.

Simon is a reminder that loss of any kind can quickly lead to jealousy and discouragement and depression and finally, bitterness. It is an event chain that is more easily broken at the earliest stages. Loss can lead to bitterness or to self-evaluation, prayer, and renewal. It was Simon's choice. It is your choice—and mine.

> Things don't go wrong and break your heart so you can become bitter and give up. They happen to break you down and build you up so you can be all that you were intended to be.
>
> —Charlie Jones

Each heart knows its own bitterness.

Proverbs 14:10a

CHAPTER NINE

CALUARY (SAME)

GOLGOTHA: MOUNTAIN OF GRACE

Behind Calvary is the throne of heaven.

—James S. Stewart

So the soldiers took charge of Jesus. Carrying his own cross, he went out to the place of the Skull (which in Aramaic is called Golgotha). Here they crucified him, and with him two others—one on each side and Jesus in the middle.

John 19:16b–18

THERE CAN BE SOME CONFUSION about the names Calvary and Golgotha, although they refer to exactly the same place. The word *kranion*, used in the Greek manuscripts from which our Bible is translated, is the word from which we get the English word *cranium*. When the Bible was translated into Latin in the fourth century, the Latin equivalent was *Calvaria*, which gives us our English word *Calvary*. And the Aramaic word was *Golgotha*. They all mean the same thing: "skull."

There are three possible reasons that this small hill acquired that name: because skulls were found there, because it was a place of execution, or because this rocky knob resembled a skull. History leans toward that last possibility. It is generally believed from the historic reports that this barren hill of execution was a bare rock, which looked something like the smooth top of a human skull bone.

All we really know about Golgotha from Scripture is that it was outside the city walls of Jerusalem, probably not far from one of the city gates, that it was a fairly prominent landmark, and that there was a garden nearby containing a tomb. The present-day Church of the Holy Sepulcher is said to occupy the site of Golgotha, but there is no way to verify that.

There is no reason to believe that Golgotha was any more than a small hill close to Jerusalem's city walls, but its significance to Christianity easily compensates for its physical size. In any discussion of what Christians believe and hold dear, Golgotha or Calvary rises to the top of the list of significant locations. It is a small hill of little or no geographic significance but an eternal and spiritual mountain of unequaled magnitude. Calvary is not tall, not pretty, and not fruitful unless you view it through the lens of the Bible. But when seen through that lens, Golgotha/Calvary becomes the soaring Himalaya of eternal spiritual value and the most fruitful mountain in all eternity with a beauty that will never fade.

> On a hill far away stood an old rugged cross,
> the emblem of suffering and shame.
>
> —George Bennard

They brought Jesus to the place called Golgotha (which means The Place of the Skull).

Mark 15:22

Golgotha was not tall. Even though its exact location today is unknown, it is safe to assume that Golgotha was not much more than a knob of stone that rose slightly above the surrounding terrain.

Constantine's mother, Helena, visited the site in 325 AD and described it as "a little hill." Golgotha was clearly not much as a natural feature.

And this is interesting because humankind has always been impressed by heights. It is a thoroughly normal reaction to look at a tall object with certain wonder and fascination. The building called Burj Khalifa (Khalifa Tower in Arabic) in Dubai soars to 2,722 feet, over a half-mile and nearly twice the height of New York's Empire State Building. To look at it is to wonder about the view from the top and the grandeur of any man-made object that high.

Spiritual monuments are often built to great heights as a statement of their heavenly purpose. Cathedrals always include massive spires to, well, inspire us.

Within a few generations of Noah and his family, people determined to build a great lofty tower *that reaches to the heavens* (Genesis 11:4). But their motives were not for godly worship but to raise themselves up to God's level. It didn't work. It never does.

The pagan people of Canaan always built their places of worship on high hills and mountains, and then used tall poles to add to that height. The Mayans of Central America built lofty pyramids on which to offer human sacrifices, and by way of contrast they believed that the underground was a place of putrefaction and evil. Height was good. Height supposedly brought them closer to God. In a sense, spirituality could be measured by elevation, or so they thought.

Still, it is interesting that many of God's special moments with humankind took place on tall mountains, the very subject of this book. He challenged Abraham's faith on Moriah. He delivered His commandments on Sinai. He chose to be transfigured on "a high mountain." And so forth.

But Golgotha was not tall. Golgotha was a mean little rock that the local people referred to as "the skull pan." Certainly not an auspicious place for man to worship or to expect a confrontation with God. And yet, for a moment in time, Golgotha was the tallest point on the earth's surface. For a moment, Golgotha was so tall that it was the very point where earth made direct contact with the one eternal God. There was and is no taller place.

> In that old rugged cross,
>
> stained with blood so divine,
>
> a wondrous beauty I see.
>
> —George Bennard

> *This man was handed over to you by God's set purpose and fore-knowledge; and you, with the help of wicked men, put him to death by nailing him to the cross.*
>
> Acts 2:23

Golgotha was not beautiful. By all that we know it was a naked rock, very likely stained with the blood and waste of those executed, and without any of the softening touches of vegetation. Just think of a very large, very dirty stone heated by the Judean sun, stinking of death and excrement. No one has ever used Golgotha as a symbol of artistic beauty because it was not. Art may be in the eye of the beholder, but there are some things that are simply and genuinely ugly. Golgotha was one.

But we all love grace and beauty: flowers, children, sunsets, seashells. We have some innate sense that longs for beauty. I have been blessed to observe many things of beauty and I am grateful for each one.

There was the morning when we awakened to see two barred owl fledglings standing on the rail of our deck. Their plumage was fluffy and puffed in the morning sunlight in a way that made them appear luminescent and surreal. These were rank juveniles who didn't yet understand that owls were nocturnal predators and not decorative showpieces. They stayed on the deck railing for most of an hour and displayed their great beauty of color and shading and shape. They were stunning, but they never came back to that spot, presumably because they learned their proper role in the world, which was to lurk inconspicuously in trees so as not to alarm potential dinner entrees.

There is the memory of autumn foliage backlighted by a setting sun in a clear blue sky. It is a scene of sensory overload with too many vivid colors on display at one moment. It is a moment for photographs or a painter's brush but, in the end, it is a moment to be frozen in memory for its sheer beauty.

There is the vista of the Greenland ice cap from miles above on a clear day when the brilliant-white glaciers shed crystalline rivulets that run down to pools of deep blue water and into an ocean sparkling with flashes of reflected sunlight—all of this against a gentle cerulean sky peppered with occasional stratus clouds.

Golgotha was not pretty even if so much of creation is. There are spring crocuses in shallow snow. Roses on a trellis. The effortless flight of a red-tailed hawk. My mandevilla plant growing up its assigned trellis and throwing dozens of brilliant blossoms out into the summer sunshine. Hummingbirds. Butterflies. The weathered face of a wise old friend. The perfect face of a child. Birdsongs on a spring morning. Silence in soft-falling snow. The sound of surf on the beach.

Beauty is everywhere, yes, but it is often collocated with ugliness. Roses dying in autumn. The blood of an elegant songbird on new-fallen snow, butchered by a sharp-shinned hawk. Trash strewn along a country lane. Blighted neighborhoods, double blighted with hopelessness. Warm family memories tarnished by recollections of sudden death or cruel accident. Beauty and ugliness coexist in a world created by God but contaminated by sin.

And that was the case at Golgotha. The hill itself was unattractive, or worse. The event was bloody and cruel and sadistic. The day was oppressed with darkness and a violent earthquake. Jesus' family and followers were crushed by disappointment and fear. It was a perfect storm of repulsive ugliness.

But the infinite magnificence of Golgotha exceeded all the beauty that has ever been created. The sacrifice of God's Son for all the sins of all time is surely the single most elegant event in eternity, and one never to be exceeded.

He who knew no sin died for all sin.

He who had no sin in Him had all sin of all time cast on Him.

And because of that, we who believe still have much sin in us but by grace have no sin on us.

Is there anything more striking?

"In that old rugged cross, stained with blood so divine, a wondrous beauty I see," wrote George Bennard.

A wondrous beauty, indeed.

> Oh, the mighty gulf that God did span at Calvary!
>
> —William R. Newell

> *They came to a place called Golgotha*
>
> *(which means The Place of the Skull).*
> *Above his head they placed the written charge against him: THIS IS*
> *JESUS, THE KING OF THE JEWS.*
>
> Matthew 27:33, 37

Golgotha, the hill, was not fruitful. Golgotha was an exposed rock where we can assume no useful vegetation grew and no water flowed. It would be the modern equivalent of an inner-city parking lot. Hard, dry, dirty, and bare. Nothing growing except for some hardy weeds of no real value. And, Golgotha was certainly not a fruitful place. In fact it was just the opposite—a place where life was taken, brutally and regularly. Golgotha was a place of death, not life. But ironically, Golgotha was the convergence of two very fruitful things, which together produced grisly death: mountains (or hills), which are normally great sources of life and vitality, and God Himself, who was the Creator of all life. But on that hill on that day there was only death.

Consider the normal situation for hills and mountains. In many places hills are desired locations for orchards since they have the right combination of moisture and drainage and because the cold air of early and late evening frosts drains down into the valleys and leaves those hilltops just warm enough to avoid freezing either the fruit or the buds. Many hills are covered with wonderfully fruitful orchards.

In the United States, mountains are teeming with wildlife: bears, bighorn sheep, coyotes, badgers, wolves, eagles, and much more. Some species have names that reflect their preferred habitat: mountain lions, mountain goats, red mountain flowers, and Alpine clematis.

If you hike mountain trails above the tree line, you will find endless varieties of flowers and evergreens that grow, even from narrow crevasses in sheets of granite. If you go higher, you will find moss and lichen growing on the surface of rocks. And comingled with all this vegetation is a thriving community of insects, all conducting their business with great ingenuity and persistence.

Mountains are incubators of life. Golgotha was a dead rock where death was the business. Further, the man on the cross was also the God who created all things. Here the author of fruitfulness died; an eternal paradox.

And yet, in a majestic and eternal and divine way, there was great fruit on Golgotha. Golgotha would yield a crop of children adopted by the living God to be His for eternity. Golgotha would reap the human population of heaven for eternity. In the end, this sterile rock would birth a populace of forgiven and cherished believers who God the Father would adopt as His beloved children.

Sounds fruitful to me. And lofty. And beautiful.

Lest I forget Gethsemane,
Lest I forget Thine agony;
Lest I forget Thy love for me,
Lead me to Calvary.

—Jennie E. Hussey

Christ redeemed us from the curse of the law by becoming a curse for us, for it is written:

"Cursed is everyone who is hung on a tree."

Galatians 3:13

PTL / / /

CHAPTER TEN

MARS HILL: MOUNTAIN OF EVANGELISM

It is a remarkable truth that the same God who worked 'through Christ' to achieve the reconciliation now works 'through us' to announce it.

—John Stott

"Go, stand in the temple courts," he said,
"and tell the people the full message of this new life."

Acts 5:20

MARS HILL IS A PROMINENT landmark in the Greek city of Athens. It is a stark granite outcropping that rises like a stone pedestal to a height of 370 feet. It is clearly not a mountain, but its significance in the history of Christianity is surely great enough for it to be included in this survey of biblical peaks. I find it interesting that the "mountain" of salvation (Golgotha) and the "mountain" of evangelism (Mars Hill) are both small, bare rock hills. God didn't need soaring mountains for His most important work. Solid rock was the best material.

The Greeks called this hill Areopagus, which means (sort of) "rock of the god of war." The Romans called it Mars Hill, which means about the same thing in Latin since the Roman god of war was named Mars.

Either name identifies the same location. It is a prominent geological formation in the Greek city of Athens.

At one time, this site had been the meeting place of the city council and the seat of government. By New Testament times, the government had moved to more comfortable quarters and Mars Hill had transitioned to an open-air gathering place for those who considered themselves to be enlightened or uniquely informed. It was a public forum like Dam Square in Amsterdam or The Boston Commons in Boston, Massachusetts, where anyone could share ideas and make supposedly profound statements. People—men especially—would gather on Mars Hill to discuss politics and religion, and share new ideas and current events. Today they would be blogging or tweeting, but in the middle of the first century, they went to Mars Hill to express their personal stories and opinions. It was social networking before printing and electricity.

Paul's missionary journeys took him to Athens about twenty years after Jesus' death. Athens at that time was the cultural and intellectual center of the world. It was a place of teaching and learning and a venue to compare ideas and develop new ones. The intelligentsia in Athens was no different than their modern-day counterparts. They were deeply attached to their pet theories and sometimes overtly proud of what they thought was their intellectualism and originality.

Into this mix came the apostle Paul, who was among the most educated of men. He had studied under the greatest scholars, spoke several languages, and had traveled widely. Paul was easily their intellectual equal, and probably much more.

Further, Paul was aware that if you wanted to mix with this scholarly bunch, you could do so on Mars Hill, where they would gather to promote and defend their opinions about their favorite gods. The Greeks had a plethora of gods, one for every occasion. Aphrodite was the goddess of love and pleasure, the goddess of sexuality. Hestia was the goddess of chastity, making one wonder how those two coexisted. Ares was the god of conflict and war and thus he lent his name to the

Areopagus (Areios Pagos, "Rock of Ares"). Zeus was the senior dude who lived on the highest summit of the mythical Mount Olympus and dispensed justice. There were more—a lot more. These Greek gods were a big quarrelsome family, intermarried, incestuous, unpredictable, and capricious. But these were the entities that Greeks looked to for wisdom and eternal security. Good luck with that.

On the top of Areopagus there were multiple monuments to these gods, along with objects of worship and altars for particular deities. It was a challenge for Greek people to pacify and satisfy so many gods with often conflicting interests, so they needed multiple shrines and pillars and statues. Any one of those gods could make your life miserable or bring you great joy. You had to appeal to all of them all the time, and the whole thing could be very tiring and stressful.

Paul intruded into that social/religious/academic environment with the radical message of one single God. He was a stranger to this well-established club of thinkers and talkers, and his audience was naturally skeptical and maybe somewhat hostile. It would have been like preaching in Harvard Square about the need for salvation by grace to an audience of highly educated, agnostic intellectuals who had cynical opinions about religion and eternity. In this current age, you can teach and preach anything in secular universities except the divinity of Jesus and salvation by grace. We have our own Mars Hills, hundreds of them.

There is no impact without contact. Evangelism is a contact sport.

—Douglas M. Cecil

Where is the wise man? Where is the scholar? Where is the philosopher of this age? Has not God made foolish the wisdom of the world?

1 Corinthians 1:20

The men who congregated on Mars Hill to pontificate on the issues of the day and the issues of eternity surely thought they were wise, scholarly, and philosophical. They were the descendants of a long heritage of Greek philosophy.

Thales of Miletus was regarded by Aristotle as the first philosopher, but Thales was badly mistaken in his assertion that all things arise from water.

Xenophanes was closer to the truth when he asserted that all things came from some divine source and that there was only one god, although he was wrong when he maintained that that one god was the world itself.

Socrates, Plato, and Aristotle—in that order—meditated on the meaning of things with conclusions ranging from all things being metaphysical to all things being empirical and practical.

And there were others:

- Zeno the stoic
- Epicurus the materialist
- Antisthenes the cynic
- Democritus the hedonist

Together they formed the basis of Greek understanding of politics, creation, being, and wisdom. Each of them had some bits of truth, but like all secular philosophers, none had the whole truth. And neither was there anyone who integrated those bits into a coherent whole as each school of thought camped out on their personal convictions and spent their energy trying to convince others as they worshiped their favorite conclusions and gods.

Into this contentious scene came the apostle Paul, who was familiar with all these different schools of thought and who had seen Jesus Christ personally and experienced the amazing and unforgettable impact of grace and mercy and wisdom that allowed him to have a fully integrated and divine view of the meaning of life. Paul had seen the truth. Paul had the fundamental answer to the questions of life. And Paul realized that "there is no impact without contact."

So, it is not difficult to picture Paul arriving on Mars Hill one sunny Athenian day and challenging the assembled scholars with something like what he had written to the church in Corinth:

Where is the wise man? Where is the scholar? Where is the philosopher of this age? Has not God made foolish the wisdom of the world? For since in the wisdom of God the world through its wisdom did not know him, God was pleased through the foolishness of what was preached to save those who believe. Jews demand miraculous signs and Greeks look for wisdom, but we preach Christ crucified: a stumbling block to Jews and foolishness to Gentiles, but to those whom God has called, both Jews and Greeks, Christ the power of God and the wisdom of God. For the foolishness of God is wiser than man's wisdom, and the weakness of God is stronger than man's strength. (1 Corinthians 1:20–25)

What Paul actually said in Athens is recorded in Acts 17:22–31:

"Men of Athens! I see that in every way you are very religious. For as I walked around and looked carefully at your objects of worship, I even found an altar with this inscription: TO AN UNKNOWN GOD. Now what you worship as something unknown I am going to proclaim to you.

"The God who made the world and everything in it is the Lord of heaven and earth and does not live in temples built by hands. And he is not served by human hands, as if he needed anything, because he himself gives all men life and breath and everything else. From one man he made every nation of men that they should inhabit the whole earth; and he determined the times set for them and the exact places where they should live. God did this so that men would seek him and perhaps reach out for him and find him, though he is not far from each one of us. 'For in him we live and move and have our being.' As some of your own poets have said, 'We are his offspring.'

"Therefore since we are God's offspring, we should not think that the divine being is like gold or silver or stone—an image made by man's

design and skill. In the past God overlooked such ignorance, but now he commands all people everywhere to repent. For he has set a day when he will judge the world with justice by the man he has appointed. He has given proof of this to all men by raising him from the dead."

Paul made an impact by his personal contact. He confronted the revered scholars of the day and implied that they were simply wrong, ignorant of the truth, and believers in foolishness. His approach was confrontational, but it was also instructive, leading the men of Mars Hill through the fundamental truths of the one true God and into a challenge to believe.

Not much has changed. Students at major universities, taught by the scholars and wise men and philosophers of this age, are routinely told that there is no God or that He is a benevolent and irrelevant bystander. They are taught that religion is tribal and primitive. In the 1970s, those students learned that the world would soon encounter another ice age. In the 1990s, they were taught that coastlines would be flooded by the rising oceans that resulted from calamitous global warming. Since the 1960s, they have been taught that there is no truth because all truth is relative; therefore, there are only individual "truths" for each person. They are currently taught that unborn babies are nothing more than extraneous tissue and that babies are not really people until they are at least one year old. They are learning that psychedelic drugs are beneficial, but prayer and worship are a sign of mental illness.

We are still living on Mars Hill. We are all surrounded by chattering scholars and philosophers who do not understand eternal truth but we . . . we poor, simple-minded Christians preach the divine Christ crucified.

America is not dying because of the strength of humanism but the weakness of evangelism.

—Leonard Ravenhill

*I will also make you a light for the Gentiles that you may bring my
salvation to the ends of the earth.*

Isaiah 49:6b

Mars Hill was the spiritual intersection where Greek philosophy encountered the eternal truth of the gospel. It was the geographic point where Paul injected the gospel into a pagan culture like a doctor administering an inoculation. That action required boldness and wisdom and individual commitment. That is the meaning of Mars Hill for Christ followers.

Our Mars Hills are at the office, in the classroom, at the back fence of our home, on the golf course, and wherever we encounter the prevailing "wisdom" of a fallen world. It is not a place of rude intrusion and coarse argument but a place where we speak clearly about our convictions and about the value of revealed truth. And that introduces an important distinction, which is the difference between "speculation" and "revelation."

The secular world is built on speculation. Scientists study and debate the nature of the physical world, philosophers search for truth, psychologists measure human behavior and debate human motives, and theologians search for some understanding of cosmic transcendental issues. We watch commentators on TV and read books and listen to professors and visit with friends, most of which is speculation, even if some of it happens to be true. It is something like Dr. Seuss' recommendation: *"Think left and think right, think low and think high. Oh, the thinks you can think up if only you try."*

But those who accept the Bible for what it claims to be do not have to think left and right, low and high because they have encountered revealed truth—absolute truth as revealed by the Sovereign God. They have discovered with Paul that:

> *"The God who made the world and everything in it is the Lord of heaven and earth and does not live in temples built by hands. And he is not served by human hands, as if he needed anything, because*

he himself gives all men life and breath and everything else. From
one man he made every nation of men that they should inhabit the
whole earth; and he determined the times set for them and the exact
places where they should live." (Acts 17:24–26)

And, these Christ followers have discovered that their personal
relationship with *"that God who made the world and everything in it"* is
possible only by His grace and their faith. There is no requirement
for stone temples and there is nothing He needs. We cannot approach
Him by virtue of our resume but only on the basis of our faith in His
grace and our acknowledgment of His supreme authority in our life
because, *It is by grace you have been saved, through faith—and this not
from yourselves, it is the gift of God—not by works so that no one can boast*
(Ephesians 2:8–9).

It is a radical message today. It was a radical message on Mars Hill.
The gospel contradicts every other religion in the world because it is
the only one that professes a God who forgives sin on the basis that
God Himself has endured the penalty for sin on behalf of all those who
would believe. Christianity is the only religion that does not prescribe
a behavioral path to appease a righteous or capricious god. It is the
only religion based purely and simply on grace and mercy.

To his great credit, Paul chose to confront that worldly speculation on Mars Hill with the revelation of grace and peace. And it is an
example for us who know this revealed truth and who are charged by
the God of grace to spread this truth to a world lost in endless speculation. We are commissioned to tell the world this revealed truth. We
are appointed to be messengers to a world that has been hijacked by
conjecture. The mission of the church is to circulate in the world and
influence the world with revealed truth.

Oliver Cromwell (1599–1658) was an English military and political
leader who underwent a radical conversion from the state Church
of England to Puritanism (evangelicalism) in his thirties. Cromwell
later led a massive rebellion against the monarchy of King Charles I,
the Catholic Church and the Church of England. This "English Civil

War" lasted several years and ended with the trial and execution of Charles I and the institution of a parliamentary government led by Cromwell, which soon degenerated into Cromwell's personal rule as "Lord Protector" of England, Ireland, and Scotland. Power leads to corruption and Cromwell was no exception.

Oliver Cromwell is one of the most significant men in English history and one of the most controversial. He reigned for a few short years and was succeeded by his son Richard for a short time until the monarchy was restored under Charles II. Several years after his death, Cromwell's body was exhumed, tried by the court, and "executed" for his crimes. His decayed body was hung in chains, and his severed head placed on public display. He was clearly a man of passion, power, and controversy, along with his evangelical convictions.

Sometime during his brief reign, there was a shortage of hard currency in England, which hampered the economy. There was a need to mint silver coins and circulate them so that normal commerce could be stimulated, but there was a severe lack of silver. Cromwell sent representatives through the country looking for silver, and they returned to tell him that the only substantial supply of silver was in the churches, where many of the statues of saints had been cast from that precious metal. When he heard this, Cromwell, who despite his many faults and cruelties was a fervent although misguided evangelical, replied, "In that case, let us melt the saints and put them into circulation."

Good advice. We saints need to be melted and circulated so the gospel of grace is spread throughout our society.

> The pressure of bringing people to Christ is God's.
>
> We can only bring Christ to people.
>
> The only pressure we ought to feel is the pressure to make the gospel clear.
>
> —R. Larry Moyer

He said to them, "Go into all the world and preach the good news to
all creation."

Mark 16:15

Mars Hill stands as a symbol of God's command to circulate in this world of speculation and spread the truth of revelation. It is the site of a pivotal moment in history when Paul confronted the secular scholars of Greek culture with the revealed truth of Jesus Christ and the intellectual world was inoculated with the gospel of grace. And their response was similar to that of people in the twenty-first century. Some sneered and others said they wanted to hear more. There will always be those who scorn the truth and those who are intrigued. Those responses are not our responsibility just as they were not Paul's. We are only charged with climbing that hill of conjecture and sharing revealed truth and leaving the rest to the God whose truth it is.

Mars Hill is not much of an elevation. It is a small outcropping of granite but a mountain of historic significance. On Mars Hill the eternal and revealed truth of God was introduced to the epicenter of Western culture, and in that sense it stands as a soaring peak of spiritual importance.

Christians must not only know what they believe,
but they must likewise explain why.

—James Eckman

But in your hearts set apart Christ as Lord. Always be prepared to
give an answer to everyone who asks you to give the reason for the
hope that you have. But do this with gentleness and respect.

1 Peter 3:15

CHAPTER ELEVEN

GERIZIM: MOUNTAIN OF IDOLATRY

Whatever your heart clings to and confides in,
that is really your God, your functional savior.

—Martin Luther

"They made me jealous by what is no god and angered me with their worthless idols."

Deuteronomy 32:21a

MOUNT GERIZIM FORMS THE SOUTHERN side of the valley in which the present-day West Bank city of Nablus is located. It is one of the highest peaks in the west bank, rising 2,849 feet above sea level and just opposite Mount Ebal to the north, which stands 3,084 feet high. Gerizim was and is a sacred mountain to the Samaritans, and over 90 percent of the worldwide Samaritan population live in close proximity to it.

In the fifth century BC, some 2,500 years ago, and after their return from Persia, there was a dispute between the Jews and the Samaritans over the proper location of the temple. The Samaritans, who were part Jew and part other, insisted that the proper location for the temple was on Mount Gerizim. Accordingly, they built their temple there while the Jews built theirs on the original temple site in Jerusalem.

Because of that defiance of biblical precedent, the temple on Gerizim was and has always been viewed as a sort of idol, which distracted the Samaritans from worship of the true God of Israel. Gerizim has a rich and glorious history, but much of it has been tarnished by the location of what was a pagan temple and what today is the site of apostate worship. And thus, Gerizim is my choice for the "mountain of idolatry" as we consider the significance of the mountains and hills of Scripture.

> There are many ways we can practice idolatry without bowing before carved pieces of wood and stone.
>
> —Bill Bright

> *"When you have crossed the Jordan, these tribes shall stand on Mount Gerizim to bless the people: Simeon, Levi, Judah, Issachar, Joseph and Benjamin."*
>
> Deuteronomy 27:12

Gerizim has been the site of at least two great historical events, one sacred and the other profane. The first one occurred very shortly after the Jews had entered the Promised Land of Canaan and subdued the cities of Jericho and Ai in about 1,500 BC. This event was ordered and orchestrated by Joshua, but it had been commanded and described by Moses before the Jews had crossed over into Canaan. It was a grand and striking event, one involving a great crowd of Israelis—and possibly the entire race. Think of an outdoor event with a couple million people, five times bigger than Woodstock.

Moses commanded, *"When the Lord your God has brought you into the land you are entering to possess, you are to proclaim on Mount Gerizim the blessings, and on Mount Ebal the curses"* (Deuteronomy 11:29). It is a somewhat vague instruction, although Joshua elaborated on that when he commanded the actual ceremony. It worked like this . . .

All of Israel with their spiritual and secular leaders stood on the lower slopes of the two mountains with the ark of the covenant—the center of their worship, which represented the actual presence of God—attended by the Levites in their midst. This was a lot of people, possibly millions of people, standing in that valley, half on the lower slopes of Mount Ebal and half on the lower slopes of Mount Gerizim. The tribes of Reuben, Gad, Asher, Zebulun, Dan, and Naphtali stood on Mount Ebal to confirm the curses that were, more accurately, God's warnings. The tribes of Simeon, Levi, Judah, Issachar, Joseph, and Benjamin stood on Mount Gerizim to confirm the blessings. The valley between those two mountains forms a natural amphitheater about one mile wide and ideally suited to echo the choruses of "amen" back and forth.

First, Joshua built an altar of uncut stones on Mount Ebal on which the priests offered burnt offerings and sacrifices. Then in the presence of that vast company, Joshua copied the Law of Moses on those whitewashed stones as a memorial. The people just stood there as witnesses (Joshua 8).

Then the Levites read the words of the Law, all of the blessings that God had promised for their obedience, and all of the curses He warned would come for failure to obey (see Deuteronomy 27 & 28). They did not omit a single word of what Moses had written. The people stood and listened and responded to each one with resounding amens! Like this . . .

The Levites say, "Your baskets and your kneading troughs will be blessed."

And hundreds of thousands on Mount Gerizim shout, "Amen!"

The Levites say, "Cursed is the man who dishonors his father or his mother."

And hundreds of thousands on Mount Ebal respond, "Amen!"

This went on until all the blessings and all the curses that God had given to Moses had been read. The valley thundered with amens from the Israelis as they affirmed the promised blessings and curses given by God, recorded by Moses and spoken by the Levites. The natural amphitheater would have echoed those amens back and forth from Gerizim to Ebal and vice versa with amplified, antiphonal effect.

It was a momentous event. It is not likely that anyone in that generation forgot that day, and surely for several generations the story of that event was talked about. It was an unparalleled affair, and it was from Mount Gerizim that the blessings had been confirmed with a booming amen!

> We easily fall into idolatry, for we are inclined thereunto by nature, and coming to us by inheritance, it seems pleasant.
>
> —Martin Luther

> *Even while these people were worshiping the Lord, they were serving their idols. To this day their children and grandchildren continue to do as their fathers did.*
>
> 2 Kings 17:41

The second significant event on Mount Gerizim was the result of the spiritual apostasy brought from the lands of exile back to Samaria, otherwise known as the northern kingdom of Israel. The name Samaria derives from the city of that name, which was the capital of that northern kingdom. In modern usage, Samaria roughly corresponds to the northern West Bank of Palestine. In the Old Testament, this area is sometimes referred to as Ephraim.

When Assyria conquered and deported the Israelites, the king of Assyria brought people from Babylon, Cuthah, Avva, Hamath, and Sepharvaim (all Assyrian cities) and settled them in the towns of Samaria to replace the Israelites. These foreigners took over Samaria (Israel, Ephraim) and lived in its towns. They brought with them their local idols and pagan practices and the worship associated with those idols. And the Israelites, while they were in Assyria, intermingled and intermarried with the local population, bringing back their idols and concepts when they returned. As a result, Samaria became a land of ethnic integration with great dosses of pagan cultures and practice mixed with their Jewishness. As the writer of 2 Kings said, *Even while these people were worshiping the Lord, they were serving their idols* (17:41a).

And, with this as the background, the second great event on Mount Gerizim occurred a thousand years after the first (about 500 BC) when this site of that original sacred occasion was defiled by an apostate temple, which subsequently defined the mountain as a pagan place of worship. The Samaritans, in all their pagan confusion, came to believe that Mount Gerizim was the original sacred mountain and the proper place for the Jewish temple. So they built a great temple on the flat top of the mountain, Mt. Gerizim, the mountain of blessings, and it thus became a mountain of idolatry. And although that temple was destroyed after 300 years, this site remains sacred to the Samaritans and a place of apostate worship. Mount Gerizim, the mountain of blessings, became the mountain of idolatry. It is a reminder for all of us.

> If we are not content to wait on God for our desires . . .
> then our heart's desire is not set on the glory of God.
> Instead, our desire has become an idol.
>
> —Martha Peace

> *"Son of man,*
>
> *these men have set up idols in their hearts."*
>
> Ezekiel 14:3a

In March of 2006 my wife, Fran, and I traveled to Vientiane, Laos, where I conducted seminars for the pilots of Lao Airlines, the national and only airline of that poor country. Vientiane, the capital city, is sprinkled with Buddhist temples. They are mostly old and run down and maintained by jaded Buddhist priests who give listless tours and ask for donations. Those temples are gloomy places with much gold gilt on the outside and oppressive darkness within. The object of attention on the inside is invariably a great Buddha statue surrounded by candles and wilted flowers and the stale smoke of burning incense. It is a sad experience to imagine that people are actually placing their hope and faith in that lump of wood or stone and the candles burning in its honor.

And yet, we all love idols. Rachel, Isaac's wife, couldn't bear to leave her parents without taking some of the local idols. In the wilderness the Jews couldn't wait even forty days for Moses to return from Mount Sinai, so they convinced Aaron (Aaron the priest, mind you!) to make a golden calf. Solomon, the wisest man, succumbed to tolerating the idols promoted by his pagan wives.

Around the world, there are countless wood and stone images that are worshiped as gods. In the Hong Kong marketplace, there are little alcoves housing small idol statues set into every building. On Charles Buls Street just off the Grand Place in Brussels, there is a reclining statue of the fourteenth-century Belgian patriot hero Everard't Serclaes. It is a brass statue of the reclining hero that is mounted on the side of a building at chest level. It is a long-established belief that rubbing the arm of Everard't brings good luck. And the arm is perpetually shiny and bright from the countless rubs it receives every day. Everard't Serclaes, the national hero, has become something of a national idol.

We love that stuff. We are powerfully attracted to alternative objects of worship. We love any substitute for the one true God: four-leaf clovers, rabbits' feet, horseshoes, lucky pennies, and the number seven.

And it is not just physical idols. We manufacture idols in our heart that become equally powerful objects of worship. Idols of the heart are pernicious, powerful, and persistent. They beckon constantly as they seek to distract us from our first love.

The human heart is a factory of idols. Every one of us is, from his mother's womb, expert in inventing idols.

—John Calvin

For their hearts were devoted to their idols.

Ezekiel 20:16b

Their hearts are devoted to their idols and Ezekiel could have added, "Many of their idols are concealed in their hearts."

It is a simple truth that we do not like. We have idols of the heart that we are prone to worship instead of the one true God. We have idols of bitterness, envy, lust, pride, pleasure, greed, prejudice, fear, worry, and anxiety. There are more, of course, but they all have one thing in common. They are the place where our thoughts and emotions and intentions go when they should be going to the God who loves us and has promised to be our tower, our strength, our protection, our rock, our fortress, our hope, our comfort, our portion, our Shepherd.

Because the human heart is a veritable factory of idols, there are nearly infinite examples. Idols of the heart are so fully personalized and customized that the variety is nearly endless.

Consider this: a young man is eager to marry, have a wife, and start a family. He has dreamed of being a husband and father and building a house and a home. Thoughts of this desire become almost obsessive, and every young woman he encounters stimulates his longing. Eventually this desire begins to displace his desire for God and his desire to please God and serve God; a wife and family become the idol of his heart. These thoughts are not abnormal or inappropriate until they become so inordinate that they begin to displace the God who has promised to provide everything he needs.

Consider this: A woman longs for a child. It is one of the most powerful and natural cravings in human experience. She yearns for the experience of a young life cradled to her breast and growing each day with promise. In time, her longing dominates her thinking and her desire for a child becomes an idol of her heart because it displaces her faith that God is good, God is wise, and she can trust Him. She wants the child at all costs, and that is the idol of her heart. Jacob's wife Rachel was so jealous of her sister Leah and her children that she cried, *"Give me children or I'll die"* (Genesis 30:1). She was so consumed with her desire to be a mother that she apparently forgot that the Creator of all life was on the job.

It is very easy to move a simple desire to an idol, and we can know when that has happened when we see that we are willing to sin to get that desire, or we actually sin when we are deprived of that desire.

We desire financial help, healing, relationships, a job, peace and quiet, and a thousand other things and any of those can become an idol. We make idols of automobiles, sports teams, golf skills, political parties, material wealth, and jobs. And some have more carnal idols: sex, alcohol, drugs, pornography, or gambling. And in the process of time, we have elevated many of these desires to "needs." We commonly say that we need them when we really just want them intensely. In the vocabulary of the twenty-first century, "need" has replaced "want."

In the Old Testament, the Jews repeatedly turned their worship to all manner of idols, which God detested. They worshiped actual, physical idols that they adopted from the pagans around them, and they worshiped idols of the heart in the form of seeking their security from foreign help. They made alliances with Egypt to help defend themselves when God was willing and able to do all of that if they had simply sought that help in faith. *"Woe to those who go down to Egypt for help, who rely on horses, who trust in the multitude of their chariots and in the great strength of their horsemen, but do not look to the Holy One of Israel, or seek help from the Lord"* (Isaiah 31:1).

In one bizarre development, they turned an historic object intended to remind them of God's power and care into an object of idolatry. That story begins in Numbers 21 when the people were openly complaining against God, murmuring about their circumstances and forgetting God's promises. In response, He sent venomous snakes among them as a penalty for their complaints. Those snakes bit the people and many died. When Moses interceded on their behalf God instructed him to make a bronze image of a snake, mount it on a pole, and raise it up. God promised that whoever looked upon that serpentine image would live; and they did and

He did. It was a great miracle, and the bronze snake became a poignant reminder of God's love and care and power.

But in time, the bronze snake became more than an image or reminder; it became an idol of worship. The Jews began worshiping the image itself and offering incense to it and 600 years after the original event, King Hezekiah destroyed the bronze snake because it had become an idol and a distraction.

The human heart is a factory of idols, even idols made from good things. Some make idols of their church or their pastor or their favorite translation of Scripture or their ancestor's Bible or a cross that has taken on more significance than a symbol.

The human heart is a factory of idols that displace that first and most important of all commandments: *"Love the Lord your God with all your heart and with all your soul and with all your mind and with all your strength"* (Mark 12:30).

What is it that causes us to withhold from God the reverence we lavish on human idols?

—Charles Colson

Therefore, my dear friends, flee from idolatry.

1 Corinthians 10:14

"I am God, and there is no other;
I am God, and there is none like me."

Isaiah 46:9b

"They made me jealous by what is no god and angered me with their worthless idols."

Deuteronomy 32:21a

Make no mistake. God is disgusted with idols. He is a jealous God, and He cannot tolerate any interference between Him and us. Idols of any kind are deeply offensive to Him—so offensive that they are the one thing that consistently provokes His anger and His threats. He hates idols. He loathes anything that displaces our faith and trust in Him.

God has promised to be our refuge, our hope, our fortress, our guide, and our Shepherd. He wants nothing to interfere with that intimate relationship. He wants His children to love Him and respect Him above all else. He understands that we have other loves and desires and preferences, and those are fine—many are even created by Him—but He wants to be sure that none of those loves or desires become our primary source of hope or refuge. He reserves that position for Himself.

Mount Gerizim was the site of a great, holy event ordained by God Himself, but at a later time that very mountain became the locus of pagan idolatry. It is a thought-provoking affair, which can be our reminder to avoid idols of any kind. Mount Gerizim is a mountain to be avoided at all cost.

> You don't have to go to heathen lands today to find false gods. America is full of them. Whatever you love more than God is your idol.
>
> —Dwight L. Moody

> *Put to death, therefore, whatever belongs to your earthly nature: sexual immorality, impurity, lust, evil desires and greed, which is idolatry.*
>
> Colossians 3:5

> *Do not turn away after useless idols. They can do you no good, nor can they rescue you,*
>
> *because they are useless.*
>
> 1 Samuel 12:21

3/5/19

CHAPTER TWELVE

ZION: MOUNTAIN HOME

It is a great comfort to a rambling people to know that somewhere there is a permanent home—perhaps it is the most final of the comforts they ever really know.

—Ben Robertson

To God's elect, strangers in the world.

1 Peter 1:1b

MOUNT ZION IS UNIQUE IN that it has moved several times. Actually, the topographical mountain has not moved, but the designation of "Mount Zion" has migrated from the "Lower Eastern Hill," which was the site of the original Jebusite fortress conquered by David and rebuilt by him, to the "Upper Eastern Hill" where the original temple was built, to the "Western Hill," which is higher and seemed more prominent to first-century occupants of Jerusalem.

If we define the mountain by its Western Hill, it rises to a height of 2,510 feet (765 meters), certainly not a major mountain by any standard. But this mountain is significant and meaningful because it is the very site of the holy city of Jerusalem and the term *Mount Zion* is sometimes used as a synonym for that city.

The early history of the mountain and its city is fairly clear. At the time of Abraham, it was apparently called Salem and was the kingdom of that spectral figure, Melchizedek, who is described in Genesis 14 as both priest and king and who is clearly an archetype of the Savior, Jesus.

Much later, it became a fortress by the name of Jebus, occupied by a truculent tribe of Canaanites called Jebusites. This tribe was known for its ferocity but not for its modesty as when they told David, *"You will not get in here; even the blind and lame can ward you off"* (2 Samuel 5:6). But they underestimated David, who conquered the mountain, ran off the Jebusites, and built his palace there. Incidentally, that passage (2 Samuel 5:6–7) is the first biblical mention of Zion, which in the same passage is also called the "City of David." Zion, the city of David the king, harkens forward to a coming King who will occupy the New Jerusalem for eternity.

But all this geography and history can obscure the more significant meaning of Mount Zion.

> We're marching to Zion.
> Beautiful, beautiful Zion;
> We're marching upward to Zion,
> The beautiful city of God.
>
> —Isaac Watts

> *"Raise the signal to go to Zion!*
> *Flee for safety without delay!"*
>
> Jeremiah 4:6a

Zion's significance in Scripture is not its location or its history. Its significance is its symbol as a place of refuge, a fortress, a home. Zion is a metaphor for that eternal place of safety and a spiritual home that will be the eternal dwelling of all those who acknowledge their moral hopelessness and claim the atoning work of Christ as their only possible salvation.

Mount Zion is a rich symbol that can be assigned several transcendent meanings, but in these few words I want to see it as an image of home—our eternal home. And the place where we are safe is our home. *"Flee for safety there."*

There seems to be a longing in human nature for home. The Greek classic "The Odyssey" describes the ten-year trials of Ulysses as he relentlessly works his way back home after the Trojan War. Ulysses— whose Greek name Odysseus means "trouble"—and his gang suffer storms, the ravages of substance abuse, the threat of cannibals, hunger, shipwreck, and the temptations of beguiling nymphs. But he eventually arrives home. The poem is nothing less than an epic story of home going and the deep ache of the human heart for that home.

The deported Jews in Babylon pined for a return to their beloved Israel. Even after seventy years of settled living by the fertile Tigris and Euphrates Rivers under the protection of the powerful Babylonian Empire, they were driven by some internal yearning to return to their parched homeland as one of them spoke for the others in Psalm 137:1, *"By the rivers of Babylon we sat and wept when we remembered Zion."* Babylon could never satisfy no matter how comfortable. Only Zion would do because Zion was their ancestral and spiritual home.

This was equally true for Jewry worldwide following the 1948 establishment of Israel by the United Nations. They came from a hundred nations where they had been residing since their dispersal by the Romans in 70 AD. During those nearly 2,000 years, they were hated, deprived, persecuted, suppressed, and massacred. They had no land, nor government, nor national standing. They should have been entirely assimilated; they should have disappeared into the gene pool of the world like hundreds of other ethnic groups. But when their country was reinstated by the United Nations, they came with simple faith and confidence in their scriptures. They came from the four corners of the globe and called themselves Zionists. They came home. To Zion.

I had a friend who flew charters filled with returning Jews for the infant Israeli government soon after its formation. One assignment was to retrieve Yemenite Jews from the barren desert of the southern Arabian Peninsula. These were primitive people who lived in isolation, unexposed to any modern technology. They had never seen an airplane except, possibly, fleeting shapes in the sky. When they boarded the airplane, they were allowed only the clothes they wore and their religious scrolls. They were leaving their homes of centuries with nothing but faith. When my friend asked one of them if he was afraid to fly in this extraordinary machine, the Yemenite Jew said, "No. We always knew we would fly to Zion because Isaiah the prophet told us so when he said, *"But those who hope in the Lord will renew their strength. They will soar on wings like eagles"* (Isaiah 40:31). The idea of going home was far more powerful than any fear of flying in a bizarre, noisy, mechanical bird. Zion was their true home and God had told them they would fly.

The prodigal son begins his youthful escapade with little thought for the value of his home. The distractions of "sex, drugs, and rock and roll" in a foreign and permissive culture blunted any appetite for the spiritual and emotional footings of home. But when those distractions were removed by poverty, his heart yearned for home; even a compromised position at home. Even just to be a servant at home. And so he stumbles on bruised and bare feet that long distance because home is where he hopes to find peace. And, he does, with a loving and forgiving father.

I have lived a gypsy life myself. I can count at least twenty postal addresses in my past, and thousands of nights in motels and host homes in forty countries and all fifty states. Each of those postal addresses has been an established "home" for some period of time, but I have come to agree with John le Carré that "home is where you go when you run out of homes." And as I run out of homes, my compass points me to Zion. Spiritual Zion, "the beautiful city of God."

The Bible takes the word 'home' with all of its tender associations and sacred memories, and applies it to the hereafter and tells us that heaven is home.

—Billy Graham

But you have come to Mount Zion,

to the heavenly Jerusalem, the city of the living God.

Hebrews 12:22a

John Bunyan's masterpiece, *Pilgrim's Progress*, is an allegory of a man named Christian, who leaves his home in what he comes to see from his Bible is actually "The City of Destruction" and walks inexorably toward "The Celestial City," which he understands is his true and eternal home. It is a picture of all believers who recognize that this brief life goes on in a world that suffers moral and spiritual decay but which can be traveled and endured to a far better destination. There is no permanent safety here. We can lock our doors, turn on our alarms, and buy a gun, but this is not our real home. Zion is our home and Zion is safe because it is "the city of the living God."

During his journey, there never is a time when Christian considers returning home. He appears to understand that The City of Destruction is not an option. He must press on to The Celestial City, which is spiritual Zion under a different name. Christian realizes that he can't go home again, a phrase that has been popularized since Thomas Wolfe's novel of that name. And although we may long for the comforts and joys of some past home, it is never really there. That home is gone and there is no way to return. We can revisit the house, but the "home" with all its emotional and personal attachments is gone.

This is evident for anyone who has lived through the last few decades. In the past fifty years, we have seen the disappearance of traditional values as they relate to marriage and family and sexuality and language and communication. Acceptable attire for church attendance has moved from suits and ties to tank tops and shorts. Family meals are rare. Bathrooms are multigender and even the language of gender has become blurred.

We have seen the explosion of social media, cell phones, texting, e-mail, and Instagram. Airplanes have replaced busses as mass transportation. Television has grown from a dozen channels to hundreds and is being replaced by Internet video with infinite on-demand offerings. Automobiles have become entertainment centers. Clocks are digital. Space travel is routine or at least no longer very special. Nearly everything we do is controlled by computers, from writing this book to harvesting crops. Soon we will be riding in self-driving cars.

Just as Christian could not go home because his home was a city under destruction, so are we. The changes that are occurring so quickly now are not all bad. Many of them I enjoy and embrace. I never did like wearing a suit and tie or working with a typewriter. But the fact is that whatever "home" I may have enjoyed in the past no longer exists. It has all changed. So, I press on to my final home, Zion.

> Maybe home is somewhere I'm going and never have been before.
>
> —Warsan Shire

> *"Many nations will come and say, 'Come, let us go up to the mountain of the Lord, to the house of the God of Jacob. He will teach us his ways, so that we may walk in his paths.'"*
>
> Micah 4:2a

There does seem to be some perplexity in the average human about our final home—perplexity and curiosity and confusion and sometimes dread. Where are we going? Is there a final home? Where is it? How can I know?

Here is an analogy that may help to illustrate the problem of spiritual navigation. Think of life like this . . .

It is as though we are living in a giant box. It is a very large box that easily holds all 7.5 billion of us human beings. All of life goes on in that box: work, play, war and peace, marriage and family, education, entertainment, worship, and all the other activities that occupy humans. It all takes place inside this six-sided box.

In that box there is constant interaction and speculation about all things. Science and arts and social studies and engineering and all forms of religion and social theories develop inside this box as people publish their ideas and findings and discuss possibilities. We articulate thoughts and then work to verify them. Some of those concepts are confirmed by controlled studies and become a part of established and accepted truth. Some are no more than crude guesswork.

And nowhere is that guesswork more subject to error than in the area of spiritual thought and study. We can talk about reincarnation, multiple gods, appropriate rites of worship, and all manner of spiritual topics. But it is just talk. All of those presumptions are just guesses. The only basis is conjecture and we are left with no clear idea of what or where our eternal home is. Inside the box we have no compass to Zion. Except . . .

Fortunately this box has a window through which we can see Zion and find the correct route. This window is a book we call the Bible. It is God's revealed truth to us. It is not all of truth, but it is all the spiritual truth we need just as the windshield of an airplane reveals just enough for the pilot to navigate. It is not complete because universal truth would never fit in a book. But that lack of wholeness is bridged by God's principle that *without faith it is impossible to please Him* (Hebrews 11:6). This window has given us adequate evidence for the journey, but it falls short of absolute proof. In the end, it is evidence that cries out for a personal verdict.

So, our travelers' guide to Zion—our GPS—is a well-known book, the Bible. Zion, eternal Zion, our home, is therein revealed along with clear directions. Mount Zion—the actual mountain on which Jerusalem stands—is merely a symbol of that spiritual destination.

Mount Zion may be the most significant mountain of all since it represents that final home where believers will spend eternity. Other mountains can illuminate the path or stand as stark warnings but

Zion is the destination. We may never be able to go back to our home of origin, but we can go home—home to Mount Zion.

> You raise me up, so I can stand on mountains,
>
> You raise me up to walk on stormy seas.
>
> I am strong when I am on your shoulders.
>
> You raise me up to more than I can be.
>
> —Josh Groban

> *But you have come to Mount Zion, to the heavenly Jerusalem, the city of the living God.*
>
> Hebrews 12:22a

AFTERWORD

I'm pressing on the upward way,
New heights I'm gaining every day;
Still praying as I'm onward bound,
Lord plant my feet on higher ground.

—Johnson Oatman

*In the last days the mountain of the Lord's temple will be established
as chief among the mountains; it will be raised above the hills, and
all nations will stream to it.*

Isaiah 2:2

GOD LOVES MOUNTAINS. HE RECOVERED Noah and his family on Ararat. He established forever the importance of faith on Moriah. He handed His holy law to Moses on Sinai. He settled His holy city of Jerusalem on Mount Zion. He was transfigured before His disciples on a mountain. In the end Jesus died on Golgotha, not quite a mountain but a prominent hill outside of Jerusalem. And He has promised to thoroughly honor the mountain location of His temple in the last days. God could have chosen to accomplish all of these events in meadows or on beaches or in plains or deserts or caves. In the end, however, He chose mountains as His preferred location and even promised that we—we who have come to Him in repentance and faith—we can stand on mountains. It seems that God loves these highlands and even includes them in His plans for our future.

But we, His creations, struggle to climb God's mountains and sometimes climb the wrong ones altogether. It is not easy or natural to climb the mountain of courage (Gilead) or the mountain of faith (Moriah) or the mountain of evangelism (Mars Hill), but He has promised that we can: *The Sovereign Lord is my strength; he makes my feet like the feet of a deer, he makes me go on the heights* (Habakkuk 3:19a).

We can climb in His strength and we can make it to the heights. We can; He said so. He gives me the feet of a deer.

But for some reason, our perverse nature entices us to remain in the valley or to climb other mountains that are displeasing to God. Why? Because *the heart is hopelessly dark and deceitful, a puzzle that no one can figure out* (Jeremiah 17:9 MSG). And part of that darkness and deceit is an appetite for bitterness (Gilboa) and idolatry (Gerizim), and probably others that are not included in this little volume.

So we have a range of mountains before us with the promise that God will empower us to climb the right ones. It is one of many biblical symbols but one that can encourage and direct us as we stumble through this "Valley of Vision" (Isaiah 22:1).

> Lord, lift me up, and let me stand
> By faith on Heaven's tableland;
> A higher plane than I have found,
> Lord, plant my feet on higher ground.
>
> —Johnson Oatman

Send forth your light and your truth

so they may guide me.

Let them bring me to your holy mountain

and to your dwelling places.

Psalm 43:3 (ISV)

ALSO BY DAN MANNINGHAM:

For more information about

Dan Manningham
and
I Can Stand on Mountains
please contact:

danskyman@gmail.com
Facebook: Dan Manningham

For more information about
AMBASSADOR INTERNATIONAL
please visit:

www.ambassador-international.com
@AmbassadorIntl
www.facebook.com/AmbassadorIntl

69273047R00072

Made in the USA
Lexington, KY
01 November 2017